Updike in Cincinnati

A LITERARY PERFORMANCE

IN CINCINNATI

Edited by James Schiff

Photographs by Jon Hughes

Ohio University Press
Athens

Ohio University Press, Athens, Ohio 45701
www.ohio.edu/oupress
© 2007 by Ohio University Press

Ohio University Press books are printed on acid-free paper ⊗ ™

14 13 12 11 10 09 08 07   5 4 3 2 1

Library of Congress Cataloging-in-Publication Data

Updike, John.
  Updike in Cincinnati : a literary performance / edited by James Schiff ;
photographs by Jon Hughes.
    p. cm.
  ISBN-13: 978-0-8214-1748-5 (hc : alk. paper)
  ISBN-10: 0-8214-1748-7 (hc : alk. paper)
  1. Updike, John—Appreciation—United States. 2. Updike, John—Criti-
cism and interpretation. 3. Authors and readers—Ohio—Cincinnati. I.
Schiff, James A., 1958– II. Title.
  PS3571.P4Z926 2007
  813'.54—dc22
  [B]

2006101518

For Walker, Hayden, and Ben

Contents

Illustrations follow page 70

Acknowledgments

For their generous support of the events which took place in Cincinnati in April 2001, I would like to thank the Department of English at the University of Cincinnati, the Robert C. and Adele R. Schiff Foundation, the Taft Memorial Fund, the Mercantile Library, the Lois and Richard Rosenthal Foundation, and the Ohio Arts Council.

For their participation and assistance with the activities of the festival, I would like to thank Janet Buening, Don Greiner, Jon Hughes, Erin McGraw, Bill Pritchard, and John Updike. For their assistance with the transcripts, I would like to thank Elizabeth Buening and Drew Shannon. Special thanks go to Andrew Hudgins for putting me in touch with the right publisher. I am particularly indebted to John Updike for the hours he devoted, while on vacation no less, to revision of the transcripts; few people, much less literary figures of his stature, would be so good-natured and genial as well as thorough and prompt, and for that I am terribly grateful. In spite of such wonderful assistance, the responsibility for accuracy within this volume is solely mine.

Some of the material from this book originally appeared in "A Conversation with John Updike," *Southern Review* 38, vol. 2 (Spring 2002): 420–42; and "The Short Fiction of John Updike," *Boulevard* 17, no. 3 (Spring 2002): 22–40. In addition, the three short stories first appeared in the *New Yorker,* and two of the three were published in collections by

Alfred A. Knopf, a division of Random House, Inc. I am indebted to Random House, Inc. and to Penguin Books Ltd. for their permission to reprint "Snowing in Greenwich Village"; to Random House, Inc. for permission to reprint "The Bulgarian Poetess"; and to Condé Nast, the *New Yorker*, and John Updike for permission to reprint "Free."

"Snowing in Greenwich Village" (U.S.). From *The Same Door* by John Updike, copyright © 1959 by John Updike. Used by permission of Alfred A. Knopf, a division of Random House, Inc.
"Snowing in Greenwich Village" (UK). From *The Same Door* by John Updike (Andre Deutsch, 1962; Penguin Books, 1968), copyright © 1954, 1955, 1956, 1957, 1958, 1959, 1968 by John Updike. Used by permission of Penguin Books Ltd.
"The Bulgarian Poetess." From *Bech: A Book* by John Updike, copyright © 1965, 1966, 1968, 1979 by John Updike. Used by permission of Alfred A. Knopf, a division of Random House, Inc.
"Free." Reprinted by permission; © 2001 John Updike. Originally published in the *New Yorker*. All rights reserved. For more *New Yorker* articles please visit www.newyorker.com.

Thanks also to the University of Delaware Press for their permission to reprint "John Updike, Don DeLillo, and the Baseball Story as Myth"; a more extended version of this essay, titled "Don DeLillo, John Updike, and the Sustaining Power of Myth," appeared in *UnderWords: Perspectives on Don DeLillo's "Underworld,"* edited by Joseph Dewey and Steven G. Kellman (Newark: University of Delaware Press, 2002), 103–13.

Introduction

The Writer in Public

While a writer's success stems from work done in private, presumably in a quiet study or office, he may at times feel the need to step outside and meet his readers in public. Readers may feel a similar need on occasion to close their books and drive a few miles to meet the author. This interaction most often comes in the form of a public reading or lecture by the author and takes place on campus or in a bookstore or library. For financial as well as personal reasons, many significant contemporary American writers annually devote days, even weeks, to this ritual, flying across the country to give readings, lectures, and interviews. Although a significant experience for author and reader, this public spectacle and exchange, which in the nineteenth century was covered in detailed newspaper accounts, has received relatively little serious print attention in the contemporary era. Well-known lecture series, such as Harvard's Norton Lectures, are collected and published; however, little to no attention is given to the visit itself, by which I mean the writer's performance and interaction with his audience.

Updike in Cincinnati is unique in comprehensively documenting the two-day visit of a major American author to a Midwestern city where, in the wake of recent race riots and an airline strike, he delivered two public readings; fielded questions from several audiences; sat for an onstage interview; participated in a panel discussion devoted to his short fiction; toured a local art museum with its curator and director; and dined with students, faculty, and patrons. The occasion for the visit was the Cincinnati Short Story Festival, a two-week long celebration of the genre, which featured John Updike, Lorrie Moore, ZZ Packer, and other prominent short-story writers, critics, and editors. During its opening two days, April 17 and 18, 2001, Updike was the featured guest, and from video- and audiotapes of his various appearances on stage, written transcripts were generated, which were later revised and polished by Updike and myself. That material, along with photographs taken by Jon Hughes, accounts for the volume you now have in your hands, and stands as a record of what transpired over those two days in April 2001.

Dickens and Twain, of course, were famous for their public performances and readings. Dickens, who had had early aspirations of becoming an actor and had performed in amateur theatricals, loved the stage as well as the adulation he received from the audience. Although his friend and advisor John Forster tried to persuade him that public exhibitions—acting on stage, giving literary readings—were beneath his calling as a gentleman, Dickens began giving public readings in 1853 for charity, and by 1858 for profit. The readings brought him considerable income; however, money was not the sole impetus. As Raymund Fitzsimons notes, "Dickens began reading professionally at a time when his literary powers were declining." In addition, he was in need of distraction from both his failed marriage and depression. The readings gave him what he required. Following a private reading that the author had given years before to William Macready, the famous actor-manager, Dickens wrote in a letter to his wife, "If you had seen Macready last night—undisguisedly sobbing and crying on the sofa, as I read—you would have felt (as I did) what a thing it is to have power." Performances also provided transcendence; after one reading, Dickens found himself so animated by his audience that he wrote, "I felt as if we were all bodily going up into the clouds together." Power, adulation, transcendence, affection, personal confirmation of his worth and abilities, distraction from worries and depression—all of these things, as well as financial motivation, were fueling that desire. Dickens needed his audience, perhaps even more than they needed him, and over roughly the last decade of his life he toured incessantly, reading while on tour an average of four evenings a week and refusing to cancel performances when ill.

Few writers before him had read, much less *performed,* their works in public, by which I mean that Dickens, working from a prompt copy of his text, which he continually revised, used gesture, vocal expression, and, most significantly, voice modulation to hold his audience's attention. His ability to impersonate and to switch rapidly from character to character was a particular strength, and his performances, according to Kenneth Benson, were astonishing: "Dickens's warmth, histrionic flair and expressiveness evoked tears, applause, shrieks, laughter, hisses, and shouts of 'Hear, hear!' from his audiences." The readings also drew enormous crowds, with lines of several hundred sometimes forming overnight and tickets being scalped or counterfeited. The public reaction Dickens elicited would be more fitting, by contemporary standards, for a pop star or charismatic preacher: the performance hall packed with hundreds, even thousands of spectators; voluble laughing and crying during his reading; fans eager to see his face and touch his hand, even on occasion mobbing him outside the hall and tearing his clothing. The reading was what Dickens lived for during the final decade of his life, yet, ironically, it also contributed to his premature death in 1870 from a stroke.

Not all authors have performed so well and memorably on stage. As magnificent a writer as Melville received mostly lukewarm responses to his lectures, one of which was delivered at the Mercantile Library in Cincinnati in 1858, the same venue Updike visited 143 years later. In those days, of course, lectures were given detailed press coverage, as evident in this description of Melville's talk, "Statuary in Rome," in the

Cincinnati Enquirer, one of at least three newspapers covering the event: "Smith and Nixon's Hall was about two-thirds filled with a highly intelligent and cultivated auditory, when the lecturer, an unremarkable, quiet, self-possessed-looking man, seemingly about thirty-five or six years of age, with brown hair, whiskers and mustache, bronze complexion, about the medium stature, appearing not unlike the captain of an American merchantman, presented himself." The reporter goes on to describe Melville's "delivery" as "monotonous and often indistinct," a view perhaps shared by the *Cincinnati Daily Commercial,* which, after describing Melville as "an attractive person, though not what anybody would describe [as] good looking," remarked that his delivery was "earnest, though not sufficiently animated for a Western audience." Obviously, Melville's unimpressive lecturing style has not damaged his subsequent literary reputation. In fact, a century and a half later, one could say it matters little whether one is a brilliant and energetic orator like Dickens or a mediocre performer like Melville. Yet it matters in the sense that Dickens's desire to perform on stage for his readers is a significant, telling bit of information that helps us to understand both his fiction and his psychology.

While Dickens was the early, towering figure of the public reading, such events did not disappear with his death. During my years of graduate school in New York City in the 1980s, for instance, I had the good fortune to sit in packed houses listening to readings and lectures by Saul Bellow, Stephen Spender, Harold Pinter, Isaac Bashevis Singer, Eudora Welty, Margaret Atwood, Raymond Carver, and many others. I should add that none, except for Pinter, *performed* his work; all simply read their writing, prefacing or following it with impromptu remarks. Although few other cities at that time could boast of having so many distinguished literary visitors, that situation changed during the 1990s. Through the corporatization of the author book tour, which sent far more writers across the country to bookshops and libraries, along with the growth of book clubs and MFA programs, the public American literary scene altered. Ease of travel and increased speaking fees likely played an additional role. Currently, one can easily attend a reading or lecture almost daily in Cincinnati, where I live and teach. Although many of these events, particularly the ones taking place at large chain bookstores, tend to be far from literary, it is possible, as never before in America, to attend public readings by a wide range of writers, both major and minor, and often for free. In addition, the university at which I teach boasts a wonderful visiting writers program; since 2001, the following fiction writers, among others, have read or lectured on campus: Updike, Lorrie Moore, Don DeLillo, Jane Smiley, Julian Barnes, Jeffrey Eugenides, Michael Cunningham, Richard Powers, E. L. Doctorow, Bharati Mukherjee, Robert Coover, and Percival Everett. The Mercantile Library in Cincinnati can boast of a similar roster of authors during this same period.

As for Updike as a public performer, I had seen him read or lecture, before his arrival in 2001, on multiple occasions, perhaps more than I had seen any other writer, largely because of my interest in his work (during the 1990s I published two books on his writings). I first attended a talk he delivered at the Plaza Hotel in New York in 1987, where he shared the stage with Mayor Ed Koch, Louise Erdrich, Peter Benchley, and Father Andrew Greeley. Koch, who had a bestseller at the time, was promoting himself and boasting, while Erdrich, whose husband had advised that she begin by describing something she had done that Updike had not, confessed to having once been a pinette, a high school wrestling cheerleader. Subsequently, I attended a lecture on art that Updike delivered at New York's Metropolitan Museum in 1988; a reading at Cincinnati's Mercantile Library in 1990; a reading at the William Penn Hotel in Pittsburgh in 1991; and an on-stage interview with NPR's Robert Siegel, which focused on golf, at the Kentucky Center for the Arts in Louisville in 1997. Though I confess to having once traveled several hundred miles to attend a college basketball game, I seldom travel more than a half hour to attend a literary reading; thus, my attendance at Updike readings and lectures usually coincided with either my living in that city or being there for a conference. Further, while my attendance at Updike readings attests to my committed, long-term interest in his work, it also demonstrates how frequently this particular author goes on the road and gives public readings. Had I been willing to drive four or five hours, it is likely that I could have seen him on many more occasions.

From those five public performances, I gained a sense of what Updike is like on stage, an experience which, perhaps, can be best summarized by Nicholson Baker in his novel about literary vocation and Updike, *U & I*. Recalling "an amazing performance by Updike" on *The Dick Cavett Show* during the late 1970s, Baker writes, "[H]e spoke in swerving, rich, complex paragraphs of unhesitating intelligence that he finally allowed to glide to rest at the curb with a little downward swallowing smile of closure, as if he almost felt that he ought to apologize for his inability even to fake the need to grope for his expression." Baker goes on to describe a scene from an early 1980s documentary on Updike: "[A]s the camera follows his climb up a ladder at his mother's house to put up or take down some storm windows, in the midst of this tricky physical act, he tosses down to us some startlingly lucid little felicity, something about 'These small yearly duties which blah blah blah,' and I was stunned to recognize that in Updike we were dealing with a man so naturally verbal that he could write his fucking memoirs *on a ladder!*" Updike's verbal eloquence, his natural grace and intelligence, and his absolute ease as a speaker, despite a very slight, occasional stutter, are probably what his audience, whether live in a hall or watching on television or film, is most aware of. One should perhaps expect this, particularly given the author's facility with language and deft use of metaphor in his writing, yet one is also slightly astonished to encounter such eloquence *live* in a library or town hall, particularly when the author is speaking off the cuff. Updike's performances are so effortless and graceful that one assumes that this is the very thing he was meant to do his entire life.

One also notes in Updike's performances humility and sensitivity to his audience's comfort. Often aware of the clock, he is likely to express concern about taking too much of his audience's time; he may even introduce a story he is about to read by stating his hope that it will not go on too long. In addition, he may poke fun at his own prolificacy or speak of his accomplishments in such modest, unpretentious terms that one would have little sense of his distinguished place in contemporary American literature. Genial and generous, he is open to questions and interaction with his audience, whether on the future of the short story or his appearance on *The Simpsons*. Unlike, say, Saul Bellow, he does not express disgruntlement or arrogance at questions, nor does he look for argument or debate like Gore Vidal. He is mostly funny and clever, though in a natural, unrehearsed way. Immediately after being introduced at a book convention in Las Vegas, he fell into a coughing fit and, while trying to bring it under control, managed to say, "I can see the headlines. American author chokes to death on his own words." Updike appears to enjoy being on stage, yet doesn't get worked up or worried about it, and seemingly does little advance preparation. When he visited Cincinnati in 1990, he asked earlier in the afternoon if I wouldn't mind bringing my copy of *Odd Jobs* that evening to his reading—even though he had planned to read from it, he had not brought a copy because, he said, it was too heavy to pack. Further, his elaborate half-hour response to critical papers by Bill Pritchard and Don Greiner at the Short Story Festival was completely off the cuff, without preparation or notes.

One is hard-pressed to find shortcomings in an Updike reading. Though eager to please his audience, he is not too eager. In both Pittsburgh and Cincinnati, he delighted his audiences by reading from fiction that was set in those two cities, yet, as I've seen on other occasions, he is also prepared to give his audience something that they did not come to hear, such as his poetry, or a few minutes about President James Buchanan. I once heard an audience member express disappointment that Updike did not have a polished, canned speech as Tom Wolfe had had the year before, but rather relied on extemporaneous remarks delivered between reading pieces of his fiction and nonfiction. This man clearly felt that Updike had not made a sufficient effort to write something special for his audience. Given the large fee Updike receives, the man may have had a point. However, and speaking personally, I often find myself more eager, particularly if the writer is verbally deft and clever, to hear improvised remarks rather than a canned talk or speech. Improvisation generates curiosity, even drama—one never quite knows what will be said or happen next. Further, when Updike chooses, in between his improvised remarks, to read from a text, it makes better sense for him to read from his fiction rather than a speech, since the former is clearly the best thing he has available.

The only issue I've had after hearing Updike perform is really a question: Why does he do so much of it? Given his tremendous literary success and annual prolificacy, he surely does not need the money. As with Dickens, other factors must be driving him. Perhaps being out in public and away from the solitary work and daily grind of writing offers a diversion and relief. In addition, getting out of the house provides experiences, adventure, potentially even new material. Many of the experiences from Updike's literary traveling, particularly behind the Iron Curtain, later poured into his Bech stories. Perhaps most significantly, however, the need to connect to an audience, to hear its praise and applause, cannot be underestimated. As the sexagenarian Rolling Stones recently finish yet another national tour, I cannot help but think that what drives them is not so different from what drives Updike: the sensation and rush of energy that come from being in front of a crowd that appreciates, values and loves what you do. Finally, an element of bourgeois professionalism may be behind Updike's touring. Just as he has mandated for himself a daily writing quota of three pages, similarly he may deem it necessary, with some degree of regularity, to accept an attractive invitation to speak. Given that he does not view himself as being out there in the world like others, say, in business, this public exchange may provide him with a sense of being productive, financially worthy, and immersed in the world of commerce. In his autobiographical short story "A Sandstone Farmhouse," Updike's narrator says of his protagonist, Joey, "He had always wanted to be where the action was." This seems true as well of Updike, who in a letter to me remarked how writing reviews has kept him tied to the *New Yorker*, New York City, and the world of print: "I like, as they say, the action."

When I began organizing the Short Story Festival and working with colleagues to select writers, Updike was at the top of the list and invited first. Once he agreed to participate, all subsequently invited short-story writers and critics agreed as well. In preparing for the festival, there was a good deal of work, which I shared with Erin McGraw, my colleague at the time and herself an excellent short-story writer, and Janet Buening, an enormously capable graduate student who then served as our departmental public relations liaison. I was surprised by how much time was spent dealing with airline reservationists, audio technicians, graphic designers, public relations people, and campus scheduling. My notes from the festival are filled with phone numbers, addresses, and performance hall facts and seating capacity numbers—scribbled in the margin are such lines as "mixer wired into receiver and two speakers" and "ICB Audio self-contained."

In spite of all the effort, one cannot anticipate or be ready for the various accidents and circumstances of time. Although the festival took place five months prior to the cataclysmic events in New York City and Washington which would later shake the world, Cincinnati was experiencing its own problems in an April which had been nothing short of cruel. Comair, the regional airlines for Delta, which maintains a major Cincinnati hub, had been devastated by a pilot strike that began in late March and was generating havoc for travelers as well as threatening the local economy. Then, on April 9, a committee meeting of the Cincinnati City Council in City Hall turned ugly and was aborted when a large group, protesting the deaths of black men at the hands of Cincinnati police, began shouting, threatening city officials, and causing chaos. Their anger was fueled by the recent death of Timothy Thomas, a nineteen-year-old African American man who was shot on the street after being chased by a police officer (the officer claimed that Thomas was reaching for a gun in his waistband, but there was no gun). Thomas was the fifteenth African American to die in confrontations with the Cincinnati police since 1995. Anger from the council chambers spread onto the streets of the city, particularly the neighborhood of Over-the-Rhine, and soon Cincinnati was engulfed by a riot: fires burning, cars being overturned, looters trashing stores. An evening curfew was instituted on April 12, and as the city braced for the funeral of Thomas on April 15, many feared what would happen next. Remarkably, Cincinnati quickly returned to some semblance of peacefulness and order. While the riot claimed no lives, few physical injuries, and only modest material destruction, it was one of contemporary Cincinnati's worst moments—images of the city in flames were broadcast across the nation and throughout the world—as well as a continuing sign of bitter racial tensions and problems both locally and nationally.

Although the riots, I suppose, had little material impact on the festival—once the 6:00 p.m. curfew lifted, evening events were again possible—they were very much on our minds that week. Having viewed the events on television, Updike called from Massachusetts on April 16, the day before his scheduled arrival, to determine how things were and whether it was still appropriate to go on with the festival. We agreed it

Introduction

was. Although the riots did not cancel or curtail any festival events, they surely cast a shadow and were, for participants and audiences, present in the air, if not always discussed. In addition, the short story, which is always given short shrift beside its towering neighbor, the novel, seemed even more marginal when placed beside the tragic death of a young man and a wave of ensuing urban violence. Yet life goes on, people get out of bed, scheduled events tend to take place, and writers continue to turn to fiction as a way of making sense of the world.

I met John Updike at his gate at the Greater Cincinnati Airport on Tuesday, April 17, around 3:20 in the afternoon (in those pre-9/11 days, one could still greet family and friends at the arrival gate). A tall man, dressed in a tweed blazer and khakis, he emerged carrying a small, heavily worn leather suitcase (he had not checked any luggage). His hair had whitened since I had last seen him—he was nearly seventy, though he looked healthy and in good shape. Relaxed, cheerful, genial, and modest, he spoke fluidly; while not soft-spoken, he is rarely loud. Walking through the airport, we discussed the riots, travel, the Cincinnati airport (the fact that it is in Kentucky), then I gave him a brief driving tour of the city, including a detour through Over-the-Rhine, where the riots had taken place. Once my duties were dispatched, I dropped him at his hotel, the Cincinnatian.

We were to rendezvous at his hotel bar less than two hours later for drinks (Updike told us later that he and his wife had given up alcohol and felt better because of it), and we were to be joined by some of my colleagues as well as critics Bill Pritchard and Don Greiner, who had flown in from Massachusetts and South Carolina for the festival. Wearing a gray pinstripe suit, Updike materialized at the hotel bar and informed us, apologetically, that he had forgotten to pack a necktie. "There's always something I forget to pack." Through a light drizzle, I led him across the street to Brooks Brothers, which was still open, where we sorted through neckties, eventually found one to his liking, then returned to the Palace Restaurant at the Cincinnatian for dinner. Updike gave a good reading that evening in Zimmer Auditorium to a crowd of about five hundred, a large audience given the fact that a curfew had been in effect forty-eight hours previous; some Cincinnatians, particularly from the suburbs and outlying rural areas, were hesitant, even frightened, to travel into the city. The event was somewhat unique in that Updike read two stories, "Snowing in Greenwich Village" and "Free," which deal with a similar subject and triangle of lover/wife/mistress, but which were composed nearly fifty years apart. His responses to questions were particularly witty. When one audience member asked about his answer to a question on *The Charlie Rose Show,* he explained that on that show "one is apt to say almost any crazy thing that pops into one's head. Charlie Rose has a way of looking more orange in reality than he does on television, and when he leans toward you his face, already long, gets even longer, so that you undergo a kind of panic." Later, he responded to a question about his guest appearance on *The Simpsons,* describing how they had asked him to chuckle, which, he discovered, took some coaching as well as multiple attempts.

After the reading, question-and-answer session, and signing (perhaps a hundred waited in line for a word and signature), Updike said he feared he was coming down with a cold, and, as I drove him and the others back to their hotels, he asked to stop at a drugstore for cold medicine. "Nyquil," he said. "I think I'm becoming addicted." It was nearly eleven, and a policeman was standing guard outside the all-night Walgreen's, perhaps a mile or so from where the riots had taken place. Minutes later, he emerged from the store, smiling, his plastic bag filled with Nyquil, lifesavers for everyone in the car, and a gift for me, his host: a green plaster turtle.

The next morning was cool, crisp, and sunny as I met Updike and the others early at their hotel and drove us to the Cincinnati Art Museum, where we were to be given, an hour before its opening, a tour of the collection. Stephen Bonadies, a museum curator, led the tour while Jon Hughes, a journalism professor and widely respected Cincinnati photographer, took photographs. A hodgepodge of buildings, wings, and galleries which recently underwent a rather stunning renovation, the museum has an outstanding collection, one of the finest in the United States for a city of its size. In particular, the museum is rich in Nabataean artifacts and has a reputable collection of nineteenth- and twentieth-century paintings by Van Gogh, Picasso, Manet, and many others. Of the various activities I had suggested in advance, Updike expressed interest in a visit to the art museum. (I should add that years earlier, at a small luncheon in Cincinnati, Updike had indicated a desire, after some encouragement from the table, to visit the elevated billboard where a local radio sportscaster, Wildman Walker, had been camped for weeks. Walker was refusing to come down until the lowly Cincinnati Bengals won a game. Updike, unfortunately, never made it there, and when the Bengals won a few weeks later, Walker descended from his exiled perch.) Halfway through our tour of the art museum, Timothy Rub, the museum's then director, joined us, fastening onto Updike and leading him past his favorite paintings, each time remarking, Updike later told us, "Now here's a really wonderful painting."

Due at the university for a 10:30 a.m. panel, we cut short the art museum tour and arrived to find a capacity audience in the intimate setting of the Elliston Room, an endowed space devoted both to quiet study and literary events, its bookshelves filled with an extensive collection of twentieth-century poetry. Jon Hughes again photographed the event. Bill Pritchard began by considering several relatively ignored and somewhat experimental stories from Updike's collection *The Music School* (1966), stories written in the "abstract-personal mode." Bill then provided a close and very perceptive reading of the story "Harv Is Plowing Now," focusing on the "daring shifts of voice" and the necessity of becoming "an ear-reader rather than merely an eye-reader of Updike's sentences."

Don Greiner followed with an equally engaging paper on Updike's much-anthologized essay on Ted Williams' last game at Fenway Park, "Hub Fans Bid Kid Adieu," which he treated as a narrative that blurs genre lines. Discussing the piece in tandem with Don DeLillo's "Pafko at the Wall," a novella about Bobby Thompson's famous home run, Don demonstrated how both narratives depict mythical moments in American history. What was most memorable, though, were Updike's impromptu remarks, which he delivered without notes or preparation. Again, his wit was in full form. When trying unsuccessfully to recall the longish title to one of his montage stories, which was then provided by members of the panel, he said, "I have all of these Updike experts here. It makes me feel relatively ill informed." Later, when asked about Pete Rose not getting into the Baseball Hall of Fame and himself not being awarded the Nobel Prize in Literature, he responded, "I suspect the forces preventing Pete Rose from being in the Hall of Fame aren't quite the same that keep me from winning the Nobel Prize. But there may be a similar taint attached to both of us." What was most appealing about his extended response, however, beyond even the humor and wit, was his intelligence and eloquence, which can only be fully appreciated when one reads the transcript. While the panel session, the most scholarly event of the festival, was perhaps unsuccessful in exploring Updike's short fiction in any great depth or breadth, which had been my nearly impossible objective, the papers, along with Updike's response, provided more than ample rewards for those present.

Following the panel session, we crossed the street to the faculty club for lunch, where more than a dozen of us, including graduate students, faculty, and conference participants, sat together. One critic, Rob Luscher, had flown all the way from Nebraska, and another, James Yerkes, who serves as webmaster of the John Updike Web site, had flown in from Maine. One graduate student told me later that Updike had to field so many questions and listen to so much talk that she feared he would never be able to finish his soup. She also told me that she had asked him about romance and marriage, and that he told her that the two were distinct and that she should read, if she had the opportunity, de Rougemont.

After lunch, Updike, Bill Pritchard, Rob Luscher, and I walked across campus, directly through Nippert Stadium and over the artificial turf where the Bearcats play football, toward the College Conservatory of Music. My interview with Updike took place in Werner Recital Hall. It was the first on-stage interview I had conducted, and though only moderately nervous, I had no clear sense of how things would proceed. By the time Updike began answering my first question, however, I saw how easy it would be. All I had to do was ask a question—I had dozens in my notes—and he would launch into a thoughtful, elaborate, and eloquent response, stringing together beautifully crafted, long, complex sentences for three to five minutes at a stretch. Had I more experience as an interviewer, I might have tried to challenge him or cut off an answer at some point, though that very well could have been the wrong approach.

Following the interview, a sportswriter from the *Cincinnati Enquirer,* Paul Daugherty, arrived and, on a bench just outside the hall, proceeded with his own private half-hour interview of Updike. The focus of that interview was golf, and it generated an article that weekend in the local newspaper, the only real journalism besides a piece in the university's daily student newspaper addressing Updike's visit. When I finally dropped him off at his hotel, nearly eight hours after picking him up for the art museum tour, I informed him, somewhat apologetically, that he had about an hour before we needed to be at the Mercantile Library for his evening reading. He was a good sport about it all, though we both sensed that the schedule had become overly taxing.

At 5:30 p.m. I met him in the hotel lobby—he was dressed again in his gray suit—and we walked three blocks to the Mercantile Library, which was established in 1835 and is the oldest lending library west of the Alleghenies. Slightly annoyed by the full schedule, Updike said he had tried to nap but that there hadn't been enough time; both of us were semi-exhausted and less than eager to be heading toward yet another event. Further, upon arriving at the library, where the crowd had not yet materialized, we realized that there had been a miscommunication and that we could have had an extra half hour or more of down time. During the lull, Updike was given a tour by the library's executive director, Albert Pyle, a published mystery writer. One of the more beautiful and tranquil spots in downtown Cincinnati, the Mercantile Library, with its tall ceiling, wood plank floors, and cast-iron magazine racks, has hosted, in its various manifestations, lectures and readings by Melville, Thackeray, Emerson, Stowe, and more recently Toni Morrison and Joyce Carol Oates. Numerous writers, including Don DeLillo and William Gibson, have told me that the Library is one of the finest and most appealing venues in which they've read.

Following hors d'oeuvres, wine, and small talk with his audience (the event had sold out in just days), Updike read the first Bech story he ever wrote, "The Bulgarian Poetess," then answered questions and signed books. During the signing, I met Updike's stepson, John Bernhard, an engaging man who coincidentally was in town on business and had stopped by to listen to the reading. Bernhard, whom Updike greeted with a smile and kiss, seemed intrigued by his stepfather's performance as well as the audience's response to it; he had not seen his stepfather do much of this and was interested in how we perceived Updike and whether or not he was like other visiting writers. It was another good reading, perhaps more elegant as well as intimate in the library's setting, and afterwards a group of us took Updike to the Maisonette, Cincinnati's famed five-star restaurant (now defunct). What I recall most about that dinner is laughter, perhaps relief that the events were now over. Updike seemed alarmed, albeit comically, by the Maisonette's prices and was unwilling to order the exorbitantly priced sole meunière, though he encouraged my wife to do so and later asked if he could try a bite of hers. Mostly he was funny. When his own more moderately priced fish arrived, he held up its elegant accompanying half lemon, wrapped in a gauze dressing held in place by white strings, and remarked, "It looks like a see-through nightie," then added, to the entertainment of the table, "Or perhaps an Amish woman's cap." Afterwards, as we waited outside for the car, everyone was cheerful, there were hugs and goodbyes, and Updike, in between thanking his dinner partners, told me that he felt good and how earlier that evening, when the crowd had begun forming at the library, he had found his second wind. "It always seems to happen that way," he said.

The next morning I met Updike at his hotel, and on the drive to the airport he presented me with an inscribed copy of his new volume of poetry, *Americana,* then handed me a British edition of Baker's *U & I,* which had been given to him the day before by a fan—he asked if I would send it to Don Greiner, who for years had been amassing one of the largest and finest collections of Updike's published writings. He also told me about his dream from the night before, which, unfortunately, I've forgotten. At the airport, I thanked him for coming, apologized for overworking him, and said that I hoped our paths would cross again soon. Friendly and cheerful as ever, he set off for his return trip to Boston, his bag packed with what he called "my Cincinnati tie."

A few days later, during the second week of the Cincinnati Short Story Festival, my colleagues and I were listening to and entertaining Lorrie Moore, ZZ Packer, and others, and in the weeks following, I began generating, with assistance from others, transcripts of the many festival events. In the meantime, I sent to Updike a packet of photographs, taken by Jon Hughes as well as the photographer from the student newspaper. He seemed grateful for the photos, though he wrote, "I seem to have an expression I maintain through most of these authorial appearances—mouth half open, as if mulling a salient point or recovering from a sharp blow to the back of the head." Later, when I sent him, apologetically, a thick packet of transcripts to revise, he replied, "Don't you think it's cruelty to dumb authors to get one to a conference, have him spout thousands of impromptu and haphazard words, and then submit for his pained scrutiny these words in their disgraceful incoherence, repetitiveness, and virtual idiocy?" I did. Yet I also believed that publishing the material was the thing to do. In spite of his justified complaints, he must have agreed, since he spent a good deal of time revising his remarks and returned them promptly.

My decision to publish this collection of materials en masse, however, was delayed. While the panel discussion and interview appeared in literary quarterlies in 2002, I was uncertain about publishing the entire festival proceedings that pertained to Updike's visit. As a critic and reviewer, I have always tried to maintain some degree of credibility and objectivity, and I feared that by publishing these materials, which some would view as homage, even hagiography, I would undermine that personal objective. In addition, while I had enjoyed my role as host during the festival, I wasn't entirely comfortable with seeing that performance reproduced in print; the critic in me wanted to be less visible and not become a Boswell to Dr. Johnson. Finally, I feared that the project would be perceived by some as too light and thin to warrant serious publication. Although these doubts were never entirely quelled, I eventually came to the conclusion that the material should be published. Given that many notable contemporary writers annually spend days, even weeks, giving literary readings and talks around the country, this long-neglected subject seems viable and deserving of attention, particularly now that newspaper accounts of these events are no longer available. At the very least, it feels worthwhile to write it all down, get it into print, and save it for posterity. Further, through video- and audiotapes, as well as photographs, we have been able to create an unusually precise and full record of Updike's visit—perhaps unprecedented in nature, and far more extensive than was possible in the nineteenth century. In addition, the manuscript provides approximately eighty pages of impromptu remarks from one of the most distinguished American writers of the latter half of the twentieth century. Some of this material may prove useful to future scholars and readers, and in its entirety the volume may engage anyone wishing to better understand Updike, his fiction, or the occasion of the public literary performance. As Updike confessed, he has wanted to be where the action is, and perhaps I, as a teacher, critic, and festival organizer, have wanted something similar. This, then, in a very modest sense, stands as a record of "the action" as it transpired over two days in April of 2001.

Introduction

Letter to Be Included as an Afterword to the Introduction

Dear Jim:

I am happy to repose in your too-generous account of my public readings and appearances; would that it were exactly so. Since you ask in the course of your description, "Why does he do so much of it?" permit me a response, though you answer the question well enough on your own. For one thing, I don't think I do a lot of it—almost none in recent years, and, overall, less, surely, than Vonnegut, Mailer, Oates, Wolfe, and a dozen poets. My reasons, as best as I can understand them myself, are

1. I may not need the money, but I *feel* I need it. For two days or, in the Cincinnati case, three of travel and amiable socializing I receive twice or more the payment than for a short story that took many days of intense and chancy mental effort to compose. "Chancy"—a story can always be rejected, and come to nothing. As long as posing as a writer pays better than *being* a writer, a child of the Depression, as was I, will be tempted.

2. I get to see, in the margins of my appearance, a bit of the country, this wonderful federal republic that it is my job to know and love. And I meet a lot of bright professorial people and hopeful young students that I would not otherwise; just the deportment and dress of a student audience tells you something about where you are. And how would I otherwise get to hang out with great guys like Jim Schiff, Bill Pritchard, and Don Greiner?

3. I began late—until 1965 or so I read in public only in a few New England venues—and was pleasantly surprised to discover that I could do it, without much stuttering. The microphone and the attentive audience allay a stutterer's basic fear, the root of his vocal impediment—*the fear of not being heard.* The speaker tries, at a cocktail party or in a telephone conversation, too hard to be heard, to be understood, and anxiety jams his throat and blocks speech. Instead, a soothing honey of attention and responsive laughter eases the platform performer's voice box, and he luxuriates in a degree of attention not experienced since his parents stopped hearkening to his first babbling.

4. Reading something aloud is a good way to test it, to see if the words do flow as when heard in one's head. My effort while reading is to pronounce the words slowly and distinctly, letting them speak for themselves. You have to have faith, in the surrounding silence as you drone on, that the listener—*any* listener—is with you.

5. I have been known to write out speeches and give them, à la Tom Wolfe, but really that seems too much effort for fifty minutes or an hour in the limelight, between the dinner with the English faculty beforehand and the book-signing afterwards. Also, it bends my mind in a crippling way; there is something fishy and forced about opinions manufactured on mighty topics (e.g., "Are public libraries good things?" and "Is the planet going to the dogs?"). My fiction and poetry are my fullest and most honest attempt to describe my realities and contribute to society's net wisdom. If reading a selected sample, with what comments occur to me, is not enough for the audience, let it go down to the Cineplex instead.

I had a great time in Cincinnati; but why is there no shrine to Doris Day?

All best,
John Updike

Updike in Cincinnati

1

Zimmer Auditorium Reading

Tuesday, April 17, 2001, at 8:00 p.m.

Campus fiction reading before an audience of more than five hundred

JAMES SCHIFF

We have people in our audience tonight who have traveled from as far as Georgia, Nebraska, South Carolina, even Maine to see John Updike. In fact, when I announced to one of my classes that individuals were flying in from these distant states, one student raised his hand, looked at me in disbelief, and said, "For a writer? You mean people are flying that far to see a writer?" While I know that some will travel far for love, and others will go cross country to attend a Final Four NCAA basketball game, it's refreshing to see that people can be just as devoted to their writers.

John Updike was in town ten years ago, which translates to about twelve or thirteen books ago, and I had the good fortune to attend a small luncheon in his honor. During that meal I learned that he had just returned from a golf trip to Scotland and Ireland, and that he would be spending the rest of the day touring Cincinnati with literary patrons, giving an interview, attending a reception and dinner, then reading from his fiction. He went on to say that he would be doing something similar in a few days in another city. While John Updike was delightful, intelligent, witty, and genial, there was something that I could not quite figure out. Here was one of America's most prolific writers, an author who has now published more than fifty volumes and over two hundred short stories, and what was he doing? Spending his days playing golf and traveling to cities where he socialized, ate rich meals, and signed books. How could this be?

A month or two later I happened to be in Pittsburgh for an academic conference where, by coincidence, John Updike was the keynote speaker. Again, as I observed, the author was attending panels, giving readings and interviews, talking to and shaking hands with strangers. It was at that point that I became convinced that John Updike was merely the front man for an underground stable of writers who were working surreptitiously somewhere in the Northeast, cranking out stories and reviews for the *New Yorker* and articles for every journal from *Popular Mechanics* to *Elle*. I figured I had a great scoop here, better than finding the elusive Pynchon. But then, later that night, it must have been around eleven o'clock, I was sitting with friends in the lobby of the William Penn Hotel when I looked across the immense room and was surprised to see, of all people, John Updike taking a break, seated alone at a table, writing. Now, for all I know he was filling out a form to order room-service breakfast, but the image was memorable: the writer, after an exhausting day, still working to get the words out and onto paper, no matter what the time.

John Updike is a writer whose work is truly astonishing, not only because of his productivity, but because of his versatility (he has written novels, short stories, poems, a play, essays, and book reviews); his range (his characters are Toyota salesmen, biochemists, divinity school and history professors, Danish queens, African dictators); his intelligence (as Martin Amis writes, Updike is "a master of all trades, able to crank himself up to PhD level on any subject he fancies"); and perhaps most importantly, his verbal precision and lyrical prose. I cannot tell you how often I have read a line of his and reacted in much the same way as I did when first seeing that Tiger Woods commercial in which Tiger plays Hacky Sack with a golf ball balanced on the clubface of an iron. Watching, you say to yourself, in the case of both Tiger Woods and John Updike, *How does he do that?* As one critic wrote many years ago, "John Updike frequently gives the impression that he has six or seven senses, all of them operating at full strength."

I could go on and on praising John Updike, but instead I'll close with two quotations. First, novelist Philip Roth, who has won his share of awards, said after finishing Updike's *Rabbit Is Rich,* "Updike knows so much, about golf, about porn, about kids, about America. I don't know anything about anything. His hero is a Toyota salesman. Updike knows everything about being a Toyota salesman. Here I live in the country and I don't even know the names of the trees. I'm going to give up writing." And William Pritchard, who is here in attendance tonight, said of John Updike, "He is putting together a body of work, which in substantial intelligent creation will eventually be seen as second to none in our time." Please welcome John Updike.

John Updike

Thank you. Thank you, Jim. Gee whiz. I think that clock at the back of the hall is wrong. I have 8:17 p.m., and I'm nervous about the time because, on the assumption that this is a group seriously interested in the short story, I was proposing to read not just one, which is usually plenty, but two stories. Neither is very long, but they have the interest of having been written at opposite ends of my fairly long career as a short-story writer. The first one, which I will read first, was written in

1956, and the last one was written late last year and was just published in the *New Yorker* early this year. They are similar in that each is about a husband, a wife, and another woman. The differences, though, I think will become evident for those who have the patience to listen to both. And even to me. I reread them this afternoon and found the old one surprising. It was the sixth story of mine that the *New Yorker* took.

I set up shop in the mid-fifties hoping to be a professional writer. I assumed that the trade and the profession existed, that there was an economic niche in this country for people who wanted to write. And I think at that point in the fifties it was still true, but just barely true. I was lucky. I was one of the last ones to catch the train before it pulled out of the station.

The *New Yorker* was very important to me, as a model of excellence and restraint and coolness. It was its cool that I liked, I think, above all. The quietness of it, the understated quality; you don't get that much in magazines, including the *New Yorker,* anymore. But I'd hoped to make a living by selling the *New Yorker* enough short stories, and the fact that I was able to sell this one, after a fallow period, meant a lot to me. It's called "Snowing in Greenwich Village," written by a young would-be writer who, in fact, did live in Greenwich Village for about a year and a half. What else do I need to warn you of? I didn't notice any trade names you wouldn't recognize or anything. You would notice that what is sexually exciting to these people might not be so to you. But this is 1956.

Snowing in Greenwich Village

The Maples had moved just the day before to West Thirteenth Street, and that evening they had Rebecca Cune over, because now they were so close. A tall, always slightly smiling girl with an absent-minded manner, she allowed Richard Maple to slip off her coat and scarf even as she stood gently greeting Joan. Richard, moving with an extra precision and grace because of the smoothness with which the business had been managed—though he and Joan had been married nearly two years, he was still so young-looking that people did not instinctively lay upon him hostly duties; their reluctance worked in him a corresponding hesitancy, so that often it was his wife who poured the drinks, while he sprawled on the sofa in the attitude of a favored and wholly delightful guest—entered the dark bedroom, entrusted the bed with Rebecca's clothes, and returned to the living room. Her coat had seemed weightless.

Rebecca, seated beneath the lamp, on the floor, one leg tucked under her, one arm up on the Hide-a-Bed that the previous tenants had not as yet removed, was saying, "I had known her, you know, just for the day she taught me the job, but I said O.K. I was living in an awful place called a hotel for ladies. In the halls they had typewriters you put a quarter in."

Joan, straight-backed on a Hitchcock chair from her parents' home in Amherst, a damp handkerchief balled in her hand, turned to Richard and explained, "Before her apartment now, Becky lived with this girl and her boyfriend."

"Yes, his name was Jacques," Rebecca said.

Richard asked, "You lived with them?" The arch composure of his tone was left over from the mood aroused in him by his successful and, in the dim bedroom, somewhat poignant—as if he were with great tact delivering a disappointing message—disposal of their guest's coat.

"Yes, and he insisted on having his name on the mailbox. He was terribly afraid of missing a letter. When my brother was in the Navy and came to see me and saw on the mailbox"—with three parallel movements of her fingers she set the names beneath one another—

"Georgene Clyde,
Rebecca Cune,
Jacques Zimmerman,

he told me I had always been such a nice girl. Jacques wouldn't even move out so my brother would have a place to sleep. He had to sleep on the floor." She lowered her lids and looked in her purse for a cigarette.

"Isn't that wonderful?" Joan said, her smile broadening helplessly as she realized what an inane thing it had been to say. Her cold worried Richard. It had lasted seven days without improving. Her face was pale, mottled pink and yellow; this accentuated the Modiglianiesque quality established by her oval blue eyes and her habit of sitting to her full height, her head quizzically tilted and her hands palm upward in her lap.

Rebecca, too, was pale, but in the consistent way of a drawing, perhaps the weight of her lids and a certain virtuosity about the mouth suggested it—by da Vinci.

"Who would like some sherry?" Richard asked in a deep voice, from a standing position.

"We have some hard stuff if you'd rather," Joan said to Rebecca; from Richard's viewpoint the remark, like those advertisements which from varying angles read differently, contained the quite legible declaration that this time *he* would have to mix the old-fashioneds.

"The sherry sounds fine," Rebecca said. She enunciated her words distinctly, but in a faint, thin voice that disclaimed for them any consequence.

"I think, too," Joan said.

"Good." Richard took from the mantel the eight-dollar bottle of Tio Pepe that the second man on the Spanish-sherry account had stolen for him. So all could share in the drama of it, he uncorked the bottle in the living room. He posingly poured out three glasses, half full, passed them around, and leaned against the mantel (the Maples had never had a mantel before), swirling the liquid, as the agency's wine expert had told him to do, thus liberating the esters and ethers, until his wife said, as she always did, it being the standard toast in her parents' home, "Cheers, dears!"

Rebecca continued the story of her first apartment. Jacques had never worked. Georgene never held a job more than three weeks. The three of them contributed to a kitty, to which all enjoyed equal access. Rebecca had a separate bedroom. Jacques and Georgene sometimes worked on television scripts; they pinned the bulk of their hopes onto a serial titled *The IBI—I* for Intergalactic, or Interplanetary, or something—*in Space and Time.* One of their friends was a young Communist who never washed and always had money because his father owned half of the West Side. During the day, when the two girls were off working, Jacques flirted with a young Swede upstairs who kept dropping her mop onto the tiny balcony outside their window. "A real bombardier," Rebecca said. When Rebecca moved into a single apartment for herself and was all settled and happy, Georgene and Jacques offered to bring a mattress and sleep on her floor. Rebecca felt that the time had come for her to put her foot down. She said no. Later, Jacques married a girl other than Georgene.

"Cashews, anybody?" Richard said. He had bought a can at the corner delicatessen, expressly for this visit, though if Rebecca had not been coming he would have bought something else there on some other excuse, just for the pleasure of buying his first thing at the store where in the coming years he would purchase so much and become so familiar.

"No thank you," Rebecca said. Richard was so far from expecting refusal that out of momentum he pressed them on her again, exclaiming, "Please! They're so good for you." She took two and bit one in half.

He offered the dish, a silver porringer given to the Maples as a wedding present, to his wife, who took a greedy handful of cashews and looked so pale and mottled that he asked, "How do you feel?," not so much forgetting the presence of their guest as parading his concern, quite genuine at that, before her.

"Fine," Joan said edgily, and perhaps she did.

Though the Maples told some stories—how they had lived in a log cabin in a YMCA camp for the first three months of their married life; how Bitsy Flaner, a mutual friend, was the only girl enrolled in Bentham Divinity School; how Richard's advertising work brought him into glancing contact with Yogi Berra, who was just as funny as the papers said—they did not regard themselves (that is, each other) as raconteurs, and Rebecca's slight voice dominated the talk. She had a gift for odd things.

Her rich uncle lived in a metal house, furnished with auditorium chairs. He was terribly afraid of fire. Right before the Depression he had built an enormous boat to take himself and some friends to Polynesia. All his friends lost their money in the crash. He did not. He made money. He made money out of everything. But he couldn't go on the trip alone, so the boat was still waiting in Oyster Bay, a huge thing, rising thirty feet out of the water. The uncle was a vegetarian. Rebecca had not eaten turkey for Thanksgiving until she was thirteen years old because it was the family custom to go to the uncle's house on that holiday. The custom was dropped during the war, when the children's synthetic heels made black marks all over his asbestos floor. Rebecca's family had not spoken to the uncle since. "Yes, what got me," Rebecca said, "was the way each new wave of vegetables would come in as if it were a different course."

Richard poured the sherry around again and, because this made him the center of attention anyway, said, "Don't some vegetarians have turkeys molded out of crushed nuts for Thanksgiving?"

After a stretch of silence, Joan said, "I don't know." Her voice, unused for ten minutes, cracked on the last syllable. She cleared her throat, scraping Richard's heart.

"What would they stuff them with?" Rebecca asked, dropping an ash into the saucer beside her.

BEYOND AND BENEATH the window there arose a clatter. Joan reached the windows first, Richard next, and lastly Rebecca, standing on tiptoe, elongating her neck. Six mounted police, standing in their stirrups, were galloping two abreast down Thirteenth Street. When the Maples' exclamations had subsided, Rebecca

Updike in Cincinnati

remarked, "They do it every night at this time. They seem awfully jolly, for policemen."

"Oh, and it's snowing!" Joan cried. She was pathetic about snow; she loved it so much, and in these last years had seen so little. "On our first night here! Our first *real* night." Forgetting herself, she put her arms around Richard, and Rebecca, where another guest might have turned away, or smiled too broadly, too encouragingly, retained without modification her sweet, absent look and studied, through the embracing couple, the scene outdoors. The snow was not taking on the wet street; only the hoods and tops of parked automobiles showed an accumulation.

"I think I'd best go," Rebecca said.

"Please don't," Joan said with an urgency Richard had not expected; clearly she was very tired. Probably the new home, the change in the weather, the good sherry, the currents of affection between herself and her husband that her sudden hug had renewed, and Rebecca's presence had become in her mind the inextricable elements of one enchanted moment.

"Yes, I think I'll go because you're so snuffly and peakèd."

"Can't you just stay for one more cigarette? Dick, pass the sherry around."

"A teeny bit," Rebecca said, holding out her glass. "I guess I told you, Joan, about the boy I went out with who pretended to be a headwaiter."

Joan giggled expectantly. "No, honestly, you never did." She hooked her arm over the back of the chair and wound her hand through the slats, like a child assuring herself that her bedtime has been postponed. "What did he do? He imitated headwaiters?"

"Yes, he was the kind of guy who, when we get out of a taxi and there's a grate giving off steam, crouches down"—Rebecca lowered her head and lifted her arms—"and pretends he's the Devil."

The Maples laughed, less at the words themselves than at the way Rebecca had evoked the situation by conveying, in her understated imitation, both her escort's flamboyant attitude and her own undemonstrative nature. They could see her standing by the

9

taxi door, gazing with no expression as her escort bent lower and lower, seized by his own joke, his fingers writhing demonically as he felt horns sprout through his scalp, flames lick his ankles, and his feet shrivel into hoofs. Rebecca's gift, Richard realized, was not that of having odd things happen to her but that of representing, through the implicit contrast with her own sane calm, all things touching her as odd. This evening, too, might appear grotesque in her retelling: "Six policemen on horses galloped by and she cried 'It's snowing!' and hugged him. He kept telling her how sick she was and filling us full of sherry."

"What else did he do?" Joan eagerly asked.

"At the first place we went to—it was a big nightclub on the roof of somewhere—on the way out he sat down and played the piano until a woman at a harp asked him to stop."

Richard asked, "Was the woman *playing* the harp?"

"Yes, she was strumming away." Rebecca made circular motions with her hands.

"Well, did he play the tune she was playing? Did he *accompany* her?" Petulance, Richard realized without understanding why, had entered his tone.

"No, he just sat down and played something else. I couldn't tell what it was."

"Is this *really* true?" Joan asked, egging her on.

"And then, at the next place we went to, we had to wait at the bar for a table and I looked around and he was walking among the tables asking people if everything was all right."

"Wasn't it *awful*?" said Joan.

"Yes. Later he played the piano there, too. We were sort of the main attraction. Around midnight he thought we ought to go out to Brooklyn, to his sister's house. I was exhausted. We got off the subway two stops too early, under the Manhattan Bridge. It was deserted, with nothing going by except black limousines. Miles above our head"—she stared up, as though at a cloud, or the sun—"was the Manhattan Bridge, and he kept saying it was the el. We finally found some steps and two policemen who told us to go back to the subway."

Updike in Cincinnati

"What does this amazing man do for a living?" Richard asked.

"He teaches school. He's quite bright." She stood up, extending in stretch a long, silvery-white arm. Richard got her coat and scarf and said he'd walk her home.

"It's only three-quarters of a block," Rebecca protested in a voice free of any insistent inflection.

"You must walk her home, Dick," Joan said. "Pick up a pack of cigarettes." The idea of his walking in the snow seemed to please her, as if she were anticipating how he would bring back with him, in the snow on his shoulders and the coldness of his face, all the sensations of the walk she was not well enough to risk.

"You should stop smoking for a day or two," he told her.

Joan waved them goodbye from the head of the stairs.

THE SNOW, invisible except around streetlights, exerted a fluttering pressure on their faces. "Coming down hard now," he said.

"Yes."

At the corner, where the snow gave the green light a watery blueness, her hesitancy in following him as he turned to walk with the light across Thirteenth Street led him to ask, "It *is* this side of the street you live on, isn't it?"

"Yes."

"I thought I remembered from the time we drove you down from Boston." The Maples had been living in the West Eighties then. "I remember I had an impression of big buildings."

"The church and the butcher's school," Rebecca said. "Every day about ten when I'm going to work the boys learning to be butchers come out for an intermission all bloody and laughing."

Richard looked up at the church; the steeple was fragmentarily silhouetted against the scattered lit windows of a tall apartment building on Seventh Avenue. "Poor church," he said. "It's hard in this city for a steeple to be the tallest thing."

Rebecca said nothing, not even her habitual "Yes." He felt rebuked for being preachy. In his embarrassment he directed her attention to the first next thing he saw, a poorly lettered sign above a

Zimmer Auditorium Reading

great door. "Food Trades Vocational High School," he read aloud. "The people upstairs told us that the man before the man before *us* in our apartment was a wholesale-meat salesman who called himself a Purveyor of Elegant Foods. He kept a woman in the apartment."

"Those big windows up there," Rebecca said, pointing up at the top story of a brownstone, "face mine across the street. I can look in and feel we are neighbors. Someone's always there; I don't know what they do for a living."

After a few more steps they halted, and Rebecca, in a voice that Richard imagined to be slightly louder than her ordinary one, said, "Do you want to come up and see where I live?"

"Sure." It seemed far-fetched to refuse.

They descended four concrete steps, opened a shabby orange door, entered an overheated half-basement lobby, and began to climb flights of wooden stairs. Richard's suspicion on the street that he was trespassing beyond the public gardens of courtesy turned to certain guilt. Few experiences so savor of the illicit as mounting stairs behind a woman's fanny. Three years ago, Joan had lived in a fourth-floor walkup, in Cambridge. Richard never took her home, even when the whole business, down to the last intimacy, had become routine, without the fear that the landlord, justifiably furious, would leap from his door and devour him as they passed.

Opening her door, Rebecca said, "It's hot as hell in here," swearing for the first time in his hearing. She turned on a weak light. The room was small; slanting planes, the underside of the building's roof, intersected the ceiling and walls and cut large prismatic volumes from Rebecca's living space. As he moved farther forward, toward Rebecca, who had not yet removed her coat, Richard perceived, on his right, an unexpected area created where the steeply slanting roof extended itself to the floor. Here a double bed was placed. Tightly bounded on three sides, the bed had the appearance not so much of a piece of furniture as of a permanently installed, blanketed platform. He quickly took his eyes

Updike in Cincinnati

from it and, unable to face Rebecca at once, stared at two kitchen chairs, a metal bridge lamp around the rim of whose shade plump fish and helm wheels alternated, and a four-shelf bookcase—all of which, being slender and proximate to a tilting wall, had an air of threatened verticality.

"Yes, here's the stove on top of the refrigerator I told you about," Rebecca said. "Or did I?"

The top unit overhung the lower by several inches on all sides. He touched his fingers to the stove's white side. "This room is quite sort of nice," he said.

"Here's the view," she said. He moved to stand beside her at the windows, lifting aside the curtains and peering through tiny flawed panes into the apartment across the street.

"That guy *does* have a huge window," Richard said.

She made a brief agreeing noise of *n*'s.

Though all the lamps were on, the apartment across the street was empty. "Looks like a furniture store," he said. Rebecca had still not taken off her coat. "The snow's keeping up."

"Yes. It is."

"Well"—this word was too loud; he finished the sentence too softly—"thanks for letting me see it. I—Have you read this?" He had noticed a copy of *Auntie Mame* lying on a hassock.

"I haven't had the time," she said.

"I haven't read it either. Just reviews. That's all I ever read."

This got him to the door. There, ridiculously, he turned. It was only at the door, he decided in retrospect, that her conduct was quite inexcusable: not only did she stand unnecessarily close, but, by shifting the weight of her body to one leg and leaning her head sidewise, she lowered her height several inches, placing him in a dominating position exactly suited to the broad, passive shadows she must have known were on her face.

"Well—" he said.

"Well." Her echo was immediate and possibly meaningless.

"Don't, don't let the b-butchers get you." The stammer of course ruined the joke, and her laugh, which had begun as soon as she had seen by his face that he would attempt something funny, was completed ahead of his utterance.

As he went down the stairs she rested both hands on the banister and looked down toward the next landing. "Good night," she said.

"Night." He looked up; she had gone into her room. Oh but they were close.

JOHN UPDIKE

I remember the late Brendan Gill stopping me in the halls of the *New Yorker* and saying, "Oh," in his very flamboyant, Irish way. He said, "Oh, what a nervy last sentence that was." It, of course, refers back to the very beginning: [reads from the story] "The Maples had moved just the day before to West Thirteenth Street, and that evening they had Rebecca Cune over, because now they were so close." So their closeness, we don't know what will happen, what will come of it. It is a tale of very young marriage: still awkward with each other, still making little missteps. And the other woman is just really a shimmer of remote possibility. She seems more vital, more adventurous. She has more adventures than the frail, snuffly Joan.

Well, let's fast-forward forty-five years and here is a short story, shorter than that one, uncollected, called "Free." What do I need to warn you about? I'll just begin.

Free

"She has such lovely eyes." The remark had come from his mother, on one of her visits to the town where Henry and Lila, married to others, lived at the time. She could not have known that her son and Lila were having an affair—one which, like an escaped field fire, kept flaring up each time they thought they had stamped it out. But Lila would have known that this was her lover's mother, and that would have injected an extra animation, an eye-sparkle, into the conversational courtesies she showed the older woman. Once, her mother had been the visitor to their superheated circle of young couples, and Henry had marvelled, looking at this stout, sixty-something woman's profile at the little party Lila gave, how a person as doughy and plain and desexed could have produced such a beauty, such a lithe and wanton source of rapture.

His mother's remark had given his illicit love a ghostly blessing, and the two women did share a love of nature—they knew the names of birds and flowers, and when he and Lila met it was often in the wilds, in a lakeside cottage that a liberated friend, an older woman, lent her, on the woodsy far edge of an adjacent town. The off-season chill, and the musty smells of the canvas and wicker summertime furniture and a bare mattress and a disconnected refrigerator, gave way to the aromas of their own naked warmth, as the lake twinkled opposite the window and squirrels pattered across the roof. Lila under him, he poured his gaze down into her widened eyes, indeed lovely, a hazel mixed of green and a reddish brown ringing the black pupils enlarged by the shadow of his head. There was a skylight in the cottage, and he could see its rectangle, raggedly edged with fallen twigs and pine needles, reflected in the wet convexity of her startled, transfixed eyes.

His mother had never warmed to his wife: Irene was too citified, too proper, too stoical. For Henry, she had been a step up, into a family of comfortably well-off lawyers, bankers, and professors, but in the small incessant society of their home her dispensations of intimacy were measured, and became more so rather than less. Henry tried to restrict his appetites to match, and rather enjoyed his increasing dryness, his ever more effortless impersonation of a well-bred stick. His mother, whose ambitions for him took something florid from her unfulfilled hopes for herself, saw this constriction and resented it; her resentment fortified him when, with Lila more intensely than with several others, he strayed from fidelity and inhaled the wild, damp outdoor air.

Damp: he never forgot how Lila had abruptly stripped, one sunny but chill October day, and executed a perfect jackknife—her

Zimmer Auditorium Reading

bottom a sudden white heart, split down the middle, in his vision—into the lake, off the not yet disassembled dock and float. She surfaced with her head small and soaked as an otter's, her eyelids fluttering and her mouth exclaiming, "Woooh!"

"Didn't that kill you?" he asked, standing clothed on the wobbly float, glancing anxiously about for the spying strangers that all these autumnal trees might conceal.

"It's ecstasy," she told him, grimacing to keep her teeth from chattering. "If you go forward to meet it. Come on. Come in, Henry." Treading water, she spread her arms and butterflied her body up so her breasts were exposed.

"Oh, no," he said, "please," yet had no choice, as he saw this erotic contest, but to drop his clothes, folding them well back from the splash, and to dare an ungainly, heart-stopping lurch into the black lake water. The pink leaves of swamp maples, withered into shallow boat shapes, were floating near his eyes when he came up; his submerged body felt swollen and blazing, as if lightning had struck it. Lila was doing an efficient crawl, her tendony feet kicking up white water, away from him, toward the center of the lake. He gasped for breath, dogpaddling back to the dock, and from this lower perspective saw the trees all around as the sides of a golden well, an encirclement holding him at the center of the dome of sky. This was one of those moments, he thought, when a life reaps the fruits that nature has stored up. This was health: that little wet head, those bright otter eyes, that tufted, small-breasted body at his disposal when the electricity ebbed from his veins and their skins were rubbed dry on the towels Lila had foresightedly brought.

But even then the less healthy world intruded. He wondered if Irene would smell the black lake on him, with its muck of dead leaves. She would wonder why his hair was damp. He was not good at adultery, not as good as Lila, because he could not give himself, entirely, to the moment, rushing forward to meet it. His mother's blessing did not save him from gastritis, and an ominous diagnosis from his doctor: "Something's eating at you."

Updike in Cincinnati

The justice of the phrase startled Henry; his desire for Lila was a kind of beast. It would pounce at unexpected moments, and gnawed at him in the dark. "Work," he lied.

"Can't you ease up?"

"Not yet. I have to get to the next level."

The doctor sighed and said—there was no telling, from his compressed and weary mouth, how much he guessed or knew—"In the meantime, Henry, you have to live on this level. Give up something. You're trying to do too much." This last was said with an emphasis that struck Henry as uncanny, like his mother's blessing out of the blue. The air itself, his illusion sometimes was, hovered solicitously over him, a web of witnesses, superintending his fate, while he plodded on in a fog.

He resigned from his church's fundraising drive, of which he was co-captain. This, and giving up coffee and cigarettes, made his stomach a little better, but it did not cease to chafe until Lila suddenly, for no reason she ever explained, confessed to Pete, her husband. Within the year, they moved to Florida; within a few more years, the word came back, they were divorced. Her marriage had always been mysterious to him. "He doesn't need me," she had once said, her eyes breaking into rare tears, while she focussed somewhere over his shoulder. "He needs my asshole." Henry couldn't quite believe what he heard, and didn't dare ask her to clarify. There were many things, it occurred to him, that he didn't want to know; no wonder other people struck him as so wise. Though life brought him advancement at work, and vacations in Florida and Maine, and grandchildren, and, with Irene's guidance, an ever more persuasive impersonation of a well-bred stick, there was never another beast; such fires burn up the field.

IN TIME, Irene died, of cancer in her sixties, and he was free. By way of his friends—those inescapable knowing friends—he had kept track of Lila, and knew that she was again unmarried, after two post-Pete marriages: the first to an older man who had left her some money, the second to a younger man who had proved, of course, unsuitable. He learned her address, and wrote her a note suggesting he come see her. It had been his and Irene's custom to visit Florida for two weeks in midwinter, staying at a favorite inn on an island off the west coast—more Irene's favorite than his. The inn smelled of varnished pine and teak, and had stuffed tarpon and swordfish mounted in the long corridors, and photographs of old fishing parties and hurricane damage; on the sunny broad stair landings stood cased collections of shells, the ink on the dried curling labels quite faded. It smelled of Florida when it was a far place, a rich man's somewhat Spartan paradise, and not yet the great democracy's theme park and retirement home. Yet since Irene's death, after the two years of shared agony, of hospital trekking, of rising and falling hopes, of resolute hopelessness and then these posthumous months of relief, grief, and alarmingly persistent absence, Henry had grown timid of straying from the paths she had marked out for them to travel.

The inn was on the west coast, below Port Charlotte, and Lila's condo in Deerfield Beach, on the east coast, above Fort Lauderdale, so it was an arduous drive, south and then east into the sun, against what felt like a massive grain in the monotonous Everglades landscape. Then the east-coast congestion, the number of aggressive dark-skinned drivers, the blocks of white-roofed one-floor houses laid out for miles on the flat acres of sand like a kind of sunbaked greater Chicago, disoriented him; old age, he was discovering, arrived in increments of uncertainty. Street signs, rearview mirrors, and one's own ability to improvise could no longer be trusted. He asked directions three times, steering away from the young people on the bright streets and pulling up alongside skittish and wary seniors, before finding Lila's condo complex; squintingly he doped out the correct entrance and where the parking lot for visitors was hidden. He was inside a three-story quadrangle, each unit facing inward with a screened sunroom. Piece of scribbled paper in hand, he matched the number there to one on a ground-floor door; when his ring was answered he had trouble relating the Lila of his memory and imagination to the tiny woman,

Updike in Cincinnati

her nut-colored face crisscrossed by wrinkles, who opened the door to him. Her face had seen a lot of sun in these past thirty years.

"Henry dear," she said, in a tone more of certification than of greeting. "You're over an hour late."

"The drive was longer than I thought, and I kept going around and around within a couple of blocks of here. I'm so sorry. You always said I was slow." From the way she held her face up and motionless he gathered he was supposed to kiss it; he abruptly realized he had brought her no present. It had been the nature of their old relationship for him simply to bring his body, and she hers. Her cheek had a dry pebbled texture beneath his lips, but warm, like a dog's paw pads.

"I can't complain lunch has gotten cold," Lila said, "since it's cold salad, chicken, in the fridge. I began to think you might not make it at all."

More than once before, he had failed to show up—some sudden obstruction at work or in his duties at home. That her anger never lasted or triggered a permanent rupture had indicated to him that, strangely, he had a hold over her much like hers over him. In her voice now, he heard hardly a trace of Southern accent, just a softening of the edges. But her manner was edgy enough; she might be one of those spoiled, much-married women who say whatever rude sharp thing comes to them, take it or leave it, as if sassy were cute. Her clothes—lavender slacks, a peach silk shirt with the two top buttons undone, white platform sandals, magenta toenails—had that Florida swagger, which women anywhere else wouldn't dare at her age.

"Please forgive me," he said, playing his courtly card, until the drift of the hand came clearer. His heart had been thumping throughout his long drive, to the point where he imagined an onset of fibrillations, and his panic had grown as he searched the blocks of Deerfield Beach, with their unreal green lawns and ornamental lemon trees. Now that he was here in Lila's presence, a step away from embracing her, a kind of glazed calm, a sweat of suspension, came over him, as it used to when Irene would take a sudden downward turn, or during those endless last nights when there was nothing for him to do but stay awake, hold her hand, and feed her ice chips. How marvellous he had been, the network of friends confided to him when it was finally over. To himself he had just been dogged, obedient to one of the few still unchallenged phrases of the marriage vows, "in sickness and in health."

He became aware, at his back, of splashing sounds. There was a pool in the center of the quadrangle of condos, and her sliding doors were open to admit its sounds, along with those of shuffleboard disks sliding on concrete, cars revving up, palm trees rustling in their antediluvian discomfort, glasses and ice cubes clinking on a tray somewhere in another screened-in room looking out on the wide shared space. A memory of Lila's little lake, her white body knifing into the cold water, brought him to recognize, as she swayed on her ungainly footgear ahead of him toward her dining room, that she had kept lithe, though the years had redistributed her weight toward the middle, and loosened the flesh of her brown arms. Her salt-and-pepper hair was cut short in this hot climate and fitted close around her tidy skull, on its supple swimmer's neck. The old beast lived, and sluggishly stirred within him, chafing his stomach; in an abrupt collapse of all the rest of their lives he felt at home with this woman, their two bodies moving phantasmally among the rush-seated chairs, the glass tabletops, the faintly musty furniture of a perpetual summer. "I always did," Lila said. Forgive him. For what? For fucking her? For leaving afterward, in his own car, hurriedly down the dirt road in a semi-panic?

Over the chicken salad and white wine, and iced tea and Key-lime pie, they caught up with enough of their decades apart. Her husbands, his spousal tragedy, their scattered children, the expectable aches and predictable exercises with which they tried to stay in shape, to preserve the sensations of youth as long as they could. They shared a vanity, it seemed to him, in regard to their physical health.

"Why did you tell Pete, and come South?" he asked at last. "Was it to escape me? Was there no other way?"

Updike in Cincinnati

It was as if she had forgotten, and had to strain to see such a distant moment. "Oh . . . we'd often talked about Florida, and then the right job for him came up. I had to clean house. You were dirt under the bed. Dear Henry, don't look so sad. It was time." As she turned her head, he remembered her mother's profile; Lila's was now identical.

LILA HAD, he saw as he watched her talk and gesture, become vulgar, in the way of a woman with not enough to do but think about her body and her means; yet a vulgar greed for life was part of what he loved. It had been direct and simple. In two hours, they had said enough; they had never been ones for long confidences or complicated confessions. Their situations had been obvious, each to the other, and their time together had been too intense, too rare, too scandalously stolen, for much besides wonderment and possession. Now, as the shadows deepened in her touching condo, with its metal furniture and mall-bought watercolors, and the westering sun reached across the rattan mats toward the room where they sat still at the glass table, having returned to white wine, a vast uneasiness seized him; he was not used to being alone with her this long, this late into the afternoon.

She stood up, firmly on her bare feet. She had eased out of the awkward sandals; the straps had left red welts on her bony blue-veined insteps. They had been tendony and blue-veined thirty years ago. "How about a swim?" she asked.

"So late?"

"It's the best part of the afternoon. The air's still warm, the kids have gone in, hydrotherapy is over." She touched her shoulder, as if to begin undressing.

"I don't have a suit."

"You can use one of Jim's. He left about three." She laughed. "You can let out the waist string. He was just a kid. He used to strum his knuckles on his abs and expect me to be thrilled."

Henry stood, pleased to be standing, once again, and without the hurry, next to Lila—her serious small mouth, its upper lip

Zimmer Auditorium Reading

now wearing a comb of small creases, and her lovely eyes, gleaming like jewels in crumpled paper, bright hazel remembrances of his mother's desire to have him live, to be a man, for her. He panicked at the invitation. "I—"

He, too, had been unfaithful, as she had with Jim's abs, with Jim's predecessor's money, with Pete and his uses for her. For two years he had lain beside Irene feeling her disease growing like a child of theirs. He had stayed awake in the shadow of her silence, marvelling at the stark untouchable beauty of her stoicism; in the dark her pain had seemed an incandescence. Toward the end, in the intervals when the haze of painkillers lifted, she spoke to him as she never had, lightly, as to another child whom she did not know well but with whom she had been fated to while away a long afternoon. "I think they might have been just kidding us," she confided one time. "Suppose you don't get to take a trip up to Heaven?" Or again, "I knew I was boring to you, but I didn't know how else to be." In her puzzlement at his tears she would touch his hair, not quite daring to touch his face.

"I'd better get back," he said.

"Back to what?" Lila asked.

To that inn Irene had loved, with its stuffed fish and nameless saved shells, in Spartan comforts. To the repose he found in imagining her with him. Since her death she was wrapped around him like a shroud of gold and silver thread.

"You were always getting back," Lila said. Her tone wasn't rancorous, merely reflective, her tidy head tilted perkily as if to acknowledge what she was: a little old lady still game to take her chances, to play her hand. "But you're free now."

Back in the front room, Henry already saw himself out the door, under an enclosed sky that was rectangular this time. It would be a long drive, against setting sunlight, through the great south Florida swamp. "Well, what is free?" he asked. "I guess it's always been a state of mind. Looking back at us—maybe that was as free as things get."

Updike in Cincinnati

So you've all gathered your impressions of those two stories, plucked from opposite ends of my life. What struck me really is that the situation is much the same. The wife is still ill and somehow still victorious. The man is still skittish. The other woman is still beautifully at home in her own skin. Isn't that what we say, at home in her own skin? Now, are there any questions you might ask me about short stories, or those short stories, or pretending to be a short-story writer?

Yes?

Audience

What responsibility do you feel a writer has in regard to either making social change or reflecting culture?

Updike

What responsibility do I feel a writer has toward creating social change or reflecting the culture? I suppose there's no avoiding reflecting the culture, and it's a good thing. Stories are meant, like other forms of writing or communication, to bring light. And a story justifies itself if it clarifies our own lives, even in a small detail; if it makes us see and feel any more sharply. I think that this sharper seeing, this extra vision which a writer brings, might work social change of a subtle sort. I rather doubt a writer of fiction is in a position to create large changes, although some books, *The Jungle,* for example, did effect reform, I believe, in the meatpacking industry. And *The Grapes of Wrath* made people aware of Depression woes, the plight of the Okies, the general need to be compassionate, and the need for a society to help its weak and afflicted members.

Of course, the Russians were much concerned, up to the death of Communism, with the responsibility of the writer to serve his society in helpful ways. But they were defining the helpful ways, and there's a danger, I think, of a writer being enlisted in somebody else's cause. In the end all you have is your own life, your own witness, your own experience, what *you* think is interesting and momentous and in some sense worth telling. I think an important arrow in the quiver of a writer is the illusion that he has something worth revealing, something that hasn't quite been said before. Beyond that, I wouldn't assign him any high social tasks.

Yes?

AUDIENCE

In an interview you were doing for the collection you edited, *The Best American Short Stories of the Century,* you said that you selected your story "Gesturing" because it reflected a time in your writing when you had a particular music, you said something like that, and that startled me to hear a writer reflect on himself that way. Tonight you juxtaposed two stories from different parts of your career, and I wonder how sitting outside yourself and being an observer of your own writing changes your writing, the way you think of yourself. How do you identify the peak of your career?

UPDIKE

I don't know how clearly you could all hear the question. It pertained to a comment I made on *The Charlie Rose Show,* where one is apt to say almost any crazy thing that pops into one's head. Charlie Rose has a way of looking more orange in reality than he does on television, and when he leans toward you his face, already long, gets even longer, so that you undergo a kind of panic. And I always have great trouble remembering what I said on *Charlie Rose.* But this young man did remember and chastised me, well he didn't chastise me, but he reminds me that I talked about one story of mine, the story I chose to include in the allegedly *Best American Short Stories of the Century,* which I edited with the help of Katrina Kenison.

24

Updike in Cincinnati

I was trying to explain why I chose that story of mine instead of some others which were available. And he was struck, the young man asking the question, by my dispassion, my willingness to seem to judge myself from the outside, and I can only say to that, that one becomes one's own critic at some peril. I chose that story in part because it recalled a moment of my life that it amused me to think about, a moment in my life I was glad to see preserved to this extent, and because it had not appeared in the *New Yorker*. I'm associated with the *New Yorker*, and the collection was heavy with *New Yorker* stories, so I leaned toward this one, which had been a little too explicit in a few stretches for that exemplary magazine, so it was *Playboy* that bit the bullet and published it. But what I liked about it, beyond these extra-aesthetic considerations, was a certain music of imagery. The predicament of a man living alone in Boston, feeling guilty, in ragged touch with his separating wife, his mistress, and his children, and at the same time, in the midst of his guilt and a really faceted life, finding a kind of bliss, the bliss of solitude in city life.

I think it's hard for a writer to know when he's doing his best. It's kind of a subconscious event, a coming together of strengths you don't quite know as your own. Strengths you try to develop are often not those which you instinctively have. For example, the success in short-story anthologies for college and high school of a story I once wrote called "A & P" is quite astounding to me, since at the time I wrote it, I thought of it as one more story I was turning out to make a living. My wife read it with a marked coolness, and yet, revisiting the story, I can see that in a sense it is more peppy, more compressed and compact than many of those that I tended to like more.

But writing is, in part, an athletic feat. It's done in the head, though you can feel when the images and the words and the people's remarks are coming easily with an effort that's not altogether your own. And, like any athlete, you dread the moment when your body and mind begin to fail you. So that, in the mid-seventies, I probably was writing pretty much on all cylinders still, and exuberantly. I mean, there was a spillover, there was kind of more than you need, and up to a point that's a nice quality to have in a story or a painting. A feeling of repleteness, of there being *plenty*.

Yes—down here?

Staying with television appearances, Mr. Updike, I turned on my TV Sunday evening and there you were, animated. How does it feel to have done a guest shot on *The Simpsons,* and how did that come about?

The question was, the gentleman saw me on *The Simpsons,* a briefly animated representation of me, and how did I feel about it. I used to watch *The Simpsons* faithfully until they changed the hour when it was shown, and it suddenly no longer fit with my domestic rhythm. So I can't claim to be a morbidly avid fan, but I'm basically well disposed towards *The Simpsons,* and was flattered to be asked to be one of the many voices that they work into the endless saga of Springfield. I was shown the script which I would have to perform, and it consisted of saying, "John Updike," which I thought I could do since I'd done it before, and producing a chuckle. A chuckle. Well, that proved to be the hard part of the performance. I went to a Boston sound studio and a young man—I assume he was young, he sounded young to me, most men have become young to me—coached me through it from an L.A. sound studio. In the full plot of all this, Krusty the Clown has invited me to write his biography—well, not invited me, but has persuaded me, and I've written it as part of the factual basis of this plot. But he is so rude to me, so slighting of my talents, that when he suffers some embarrassment at a child's hands, I chuckle. So how do you chuckle over a microphone three thousand miles to make it worthy of *The Simpsons*? That was tough. I chuckled one way [Updike chuckles]. I chuckled another way [Updike chuckles again]. But always the young man wasn't quite satisfied with the chuckle and he kept saying, "Can you do this?" And then he did a really good chuckle but it wasn't mine. It turns out your chuckle muscles are fairly limited; or I couldn't do his chuckle, so I felt the session had been a failure. Yet when I watched it on television I thought my chuckle came out adequately, and I was pleased. It was the kind of invitation to which you can't say no. I did notice that both Amy Tan and Stephen King got many more lines in that episode than I did.

Were there any more questions? I've been sort of looking straight ahead. Yes—back there, gray sweater.

AUDIENCE

Could you elaborate on changes in the economics of the fiction-writing business since 1956? And has that effected changes in the type of writing done today?

UPDIKE

The question was, could I talk about the economics of the fiction writing business from 1956 to today, and what changes have been effected. There's a lot I don't know. All I know is that, in my own life experience, when I began to write short fiction and try to sell it to magazines there were a number of middle-class, general magazines, so-called, that did pay for fiction. The *Post* and *Collier's* still existed; the *Post* was a ghost of its former self but, nevertheless, it was there, and I sold a couple of early stories to both those magazines. But the *New Yorker* was the main object of desire, and it ran between two and four short stories a week, so it was a healthy market. And I think they were very receptive to anybody who was productive because they needed product.

The magazines that I mentioned above have faded. The *Atlantic Monthly, Harper's,* and *Playboy* are all monthlies and to some extent take up the slack. That is, they're quality magazines, especially the first two, that will run distinguished or serious fiction. But it's hardly a living, whereas one *could* make a living out of *New Yorker* fiction. I did, and John Cheever did, and a number of other writers did. It related, I think, as much to the fifties dollar—how far the fifties dollar went, as opposed to the nineties dollar. I certainly could not now set up shop with a family, even in a low-overhead small town, and expect to make a living from short fiction.

What the short-story writer of today can do, I don't quite know. There are these diminished markets. However, knowing that they're diminished, somebody has to feed them, somebody has to appear in print, somebody has to supply what appetite remains for short fiction. And a number of academic and scholarly quarterlies have come along, as well as hopeful enterprises like *Glimmer Train.* When I talk to young writers, which isn't often, I'm sometimes surprised by how indifferent they are to the matter of getting into print, as if the little audience of the writing workshop, the writing seminar is enough. But my crude generation thought the idea was to get into print and get some money out of it. A country as large and as literate and rich as this one should be able to support a few writers. There are still ways to make a living as a writer; I'm not sure if short stories are among them. But, nevertheless, it can be a piece of your career, and they are exciting to write, challenging to write. In some ways, you'd think that our shrinking attention span and available time would make them more attractive than ever, but reports vary on how well short stories do when bound into book form.

When I set out as a freelancer I vowed that every other book would be a novel; the ones in between could be collections and short stories. It was thought then that there wasn't any money in collections. But actually, some short-story writers have done quite well. Lorrie Moore, who you can hear next week, I would hope has done quite well with her books of short stories, as has Alice Munro; and Ray Carver before he died certainly had achieved an audience without the novel crutch. To me the novel hasn't been a crutch. It's been the main adventure, in a way. Although I've been told both as a young and an old man that my short stories are the best thing I do.

Anybody over here? Are we tired of this session? Yes—

AUDIENCE

When writing short stories, do you use pen to paper or a word processor, and in both do you notice a style change in your writing?

UPDIKE

It's a good question. When I write short stories, do I notice a style change depending on whether I use a word processor or pencil and paper? Because, I guess, I saw them as bread and butter of a sort, I've always typed the short stories. And now I always write them on the word processor. The novels are quite another story. I may have typed some; *Rabbit Redux*, I think, was typed, and *The Poorhouse Fair*. But, basically, I've always written novels by hand because the spell seemed so delicate and so important that I should have nothing distracting, even the sound of a machine, in my ears. Poems and novels needed to be written by hand. How this changes your style, I don't know. I have this belief that in certain circumstances you just think more freely with pencil and paper than you do with a typewriter, but I must say in reading the works aloud I don't see much difference. It's the same gray cells; it's the same set of experiences that I'm drawing on. But I would advise anybody who feels blocked or stymied to try to switch to pencil and paper, or pen and paper, as being the most aboriginal and most basic way of putting your thoughts on paper.

James Joyce, who wrote everything by hand and had typists at his beck and call, which many of us don't have, had a Jesuit-trained handwriting which was pretty legible. If you look at Joyce's proofs you can read them, unlike, say, Proust's. Joyce said he liked to feel everything flow through his wrist. So, yes, there is something to be said for writing by hand, but it leaves you with a lot of handwriting which is hard for even you to decipher.

Yes?

AUDIENCE

Would you care to comment on Nicholson Baker's *U and I*?

JOHN UPDIKE

Would I care to comment on Nicholson Baker's *U and I*? The U is the letter U and it means not you, but me. It was a book that arrived in photocopied manuscript in my home, and it lay there for a while because I was trying to finish something of my own and didn't want to distract myself. But when I did read it, I found it to be a very amusing, flattering, and harmless kind of postmodern homage, which I was happy to have. I've been in touch with Baker since he wrote it. I count him as one of my literary friends and a writer whom I admire, and I hope not only because he wrote the homage to me.

It was a curious book. Those of you who've read it, those few may know that in it he confesses to not having read most of my work. He gives a very long list of books of mine that he hasn't read. So it's not your standard homage. It's really an account of how a young writer relates to an older writer in terms of figuring out what a writer is. He takes an interest in things like dedications, and how acknowledgments are phrased. This kind of small maneuver fascinates someone setting out on the same track. The way he regarded me, I regarded Thurber and those other writers whom I adored and hoped to emulate. But you can't precisely emulate your models. Often nobody knows who your models are because your own experience and your own voice are so different from theirs. But you do learn something, you do learn how to go about it, how to be, as I've said it, a writer. I don't want to hold you here for all night. Maybe one more question. Right here, yes?

AUDIENCE

It really isn't a question. I don't want to slight either the short stories or the novels, which have given me great pleasure over the years. But I really do think one of the most interesting things you've given us is your essays and your treatment of other writers, your views, your comments on art. You've been so generous giving us these huge anthologies, which we can just rustle through and relax with, reading whatever we want. I just want to say that I'm very grateful for that.

UPDIKE

Thank you. I don't know if the audience could hear that. It was more homage, as if I haven't had enough, this time to the essays and the criticism. I never set out to be an essayist or critic. My mother didn't raise me to be one. My notion of being a writer was that you write the stuff—fiction, poetry, whatever; you invent and you don't waste your energy on criticism. But then when I began to receive criticism in the press, it seemed to me that I could do better than this. So I volunteered in effect to William Shawn, the then-editor of the *New Yorker*, to try a few reviews, and he agreed. At first I did them now and then, and then now and then became pretty often, and then pretty often became very often, until it seemed to me I was on the point of becoming a reviewer mainly and a fiction writer as a hobby. It was alarming. It was a monster I never meant to bring out of the bottle.

At its best, writing a review, an appreciative one, is an exercise in self-education and an exercise in organized thinking. Both are worthy enough, and I've enjoyed writing some of the reviews. If I were a real man of character, I'd probably someday try to anthologize them—boil the several quite large books down to a selected criticism. But my attitude towards criticism and essays has been that above a certain level they are all equally valid, depending on what interests the reader. And so I have, as you say, produced quite large books of the collected reviews. I would hope to review less as my energy dwindles, to do fewer reviews and concentrate on the more poetic, subjective, egoistic arts.

Thank you very much for coming tonight.

Elliston

Room

Panel

Updike,
His Critics, and
His Short Fiction

Wednesday, April 18, 2001, at 10:30 a.m.

James Schiff, Introduction

W. H. Pritchard, "Updike Experimenting: The Music School"

Donald Greiner, "John Updike, Don DeLillo, and the Baseball Story as Myth"

John Updike, Response

Campus panel discussion before a capacity audience of seventy-five

JAMES SCHIFF

Our panel this morning unites John Updike with several of his critics. As you know, the relationship between writer and critic is not always genial. Those familiar with John Updike's short story "Bech Noir" may recall how the prominent writer Henry Bech wakes one morning to read of the death of a critic who once wrote, "Strive and squirm as he will, Bech will never, never be touched by the American sublime." Bech, of course, is delighted with the critic's death. So much so that he begins a crusade to do away with those critics who, over time, have attacked his work. The critic who called his writing "prolix and *voulu,*" he pushes into an oncoming train. The reviewer who referred to his prose as "flimsy, the nowhere song of a nowhere man," he poisons with hydrocyanic acid. And the critic who called Bech "the embodiment of everything retrograde and unenlightened in pre-electronic American letters" is cleverly pushed toward suicide through a subliminal computer virus.

So it may, perhaps, be unwise to bring John Updike together with his critics; however, I have found him always to be a genial and gracious man. I also recognize that Bech's homicidal attack on his critics is purely a work of fiction. Or at least I assume it is. Furthermore, our distinguished panel of critics assembled today has long been admiring of John Updike's work, often describing that body of writing in words reserved for that which is the very finest in literature.

I organized this panel for one simple reason. While John Updike has received as much if not more attention than any living writer, that attention has focused on his novels. His short fiction, as far as I'm concerned, has not been adequately recognized or discussed, which is surely not the fault of our panel. In fact, this panel, along with one or two members of our audience today, have written more splendidly and perceptively about John Updike's short stories than anyone else.

I'd like to introduce my three fellow panelists. A man who writes with exceptional clarity and grace, William Pritchard is one of our nation's most distinguished literary critics. You probably have read his reviews in the *New York Times Book Review* and the *Hudson Review*. Since 1958 he has taught at Amherst College, where he is the Henry Clay Folger Professor of English. He has written or edited fifteen books, including significant works on Robert Frost and John Updike.

Donald Greiner is the Associate Provost and Dean of Undergraduate Affairs at the University of South Carolina, where he is also Carolina Distinguished Professor of English. Don has written or edited approximately fifteen books on such writers as Robert Frost, John Hawkes, and John Updike. His volumes, *John Updike's Novels* and *The Other John Updike*, continue, nearly twenty years after publication, to be among the most useful works on Updike.

Finally, John Updike surely needs no introduction, though I will say, in brief, that he is the author of more than fifty books, including thirteen collections of short stories. His stories have appeared in the annual editions of *The Best American Short Stories* and *The O. Henry Prize Stories* on more than twenty-five occasions. In addition, John Updike recently edited the massive *Best American Short Stories of the Century*, a volume which he referred to last night as "The Allegedly Best American Short Stories of the Century." I will leave continued praise and scrutiny of John Updike's work to our guests, Bill and Don. Bill.

Updike Experimenting: *The Music School*

Wᴵᴸᴸᴵᴀᴍ H. Pʀᴵᴛᴄʜᴀʀᴅ

My impression is that John Updike's 1966 collection of twenty stories, *The Music School*, is his most hazily remembered volume of short fiction. Although it contains one example of what we may call "Pennsylvania" stories and two of what he later called Maples stories, it doesn't have the memorable authority of *Pigeon Feathers* or *Olinger Stories* or *Too Far to Go*, volumes each with a strong inner thematic continuity. By contrast, *The Music School* is varied and diffuse: it contains what we may call, in addition to the Pennsylvania and Maples ones, a Harvard story ("The Christian Roommates"), the first Bech story ("The Bulgarian Poetess"), an England story ("A

Madman"), a Caribbean story ("At a Bar in Charlotte Amalie"), stories about a marriage in trouble ("Avec la Bebe-sitter," "My Lover Has Dirty Fingernails," "The Rescue"), a Tarbox meditation ("The Indian") and a family reunion meditation ("The Meadow"), a riff on Tristan and Isolde ("Four Sides of One Story"), and a powerful, sui generis story ("The Hermit"). It is to the remaining six stories in the volume that my title "Updike Experimenting" refers and that I'll investigate this morning. However significant they are in the overall sense or estimate of Updike's oeuvre in short fiction, they seem to me arguably the least taken-account-of corner in a prolific output.

I have support in this effort from the writer himself, who when asked in 1974 to select his favorite short story from his work, chose "Leaves," an example of what he called his "abstract personal mode, not a favorite with my critics." In putting forth "Leaves" as his "best," Updike speaks rather tartly of his choice as "an opportunity to rectify the slights of a harsh and nasty world." This mock-wounded language doesn't conceal his annoyance at a reviewer of *The Music School* (Robie Macauley) who spoke of the stories as "lace-making." Updike writes, in defense of that story, "Well, if 'Leaves' is lace, it is taut and symmetrical lace, with scarce a loose thread." "It was written," he continues, "in 1962, after long silence, swiftly, unerringly as a sleepwalker walks. No memory of any revision mars my backward impression of it." I don't recall another occasion on which the writer comes to such strong defense of one of his creations, and it suggests to me that the "abstract-personal" mode in which "Leaves" and its five companion stories were written was for Updike a deep and respected one.

The six stories in order of composition are: "Leaves," "The Stare," "The Morning," "Harv Is Plowing Now," "The Music School," and "The Dark." Three of them are in first person, the others in third. In their background, or so I like to think, is the final story in *Pigeon Feathers,* "Packed Dirt, Churchgoing, a Dying Cat, a Traded Car," which, Updike tells us in selecting it as his best for another anthology, "was written at a time when my wits seemed sunk

in a bog of anxiety and my customary doubts that I could write another word appeared unusually well justified." "Packed Dirt" ends
triumphantly, with the man arrived home in Massachusetts after
visiting his ill father in a Pennsylvania hospital, and there is a memorable glow about the trip back, his last "fling" with the old car
about to be traded in. Driving that car, David Kern experiences a
transcendent moment: "We climbed through a space fretted by
scattered brilliance and bathed in a monotonous wind. . . . I lost,
first, heart, then head, and finally any sense of my body . . . , but
the car, though its soul the driver had died, maintained steady forward motion, and completed the endless journey safely." Then he
is home, amidst the stars, "frozen in place" above his backyard.

No such moment of release occurs in the darker orbit within
which the six *Music School* stories move. Their titles, certainly of
four of them, seem deliberately blank, unrevealing—"Leaves,"
"The Stare," "The Morning," "The Dark." Their specified places
are pretty unspecified: a house on the marsh where the man in
"Leaves" spills out his fabric; a room in a city where the student
in "Morning" does his meditation; an anonymous bed where the
anonymous fellow in "The Dark" suffers his insomnia. The landscape is mainly inner and oddly lighted—"the inner darkness
where guilt is the sun" as the man in "Leaves" puts it. There is little or no "action" in the traditional sense of characters moving
about, interacting in dramatic situations, learning from experience, and redefining themselves. The stories do not have a proper
beginning, middle, and end the way, say, other ones in the volumes—like "The Christian Roommates" or "The Hermit"—have. All
the action is verbal action, with attention directed to the literary
performance taking place before our eyes and ears in the sentences and paragraphs, the "moves" of the writer. Sometimes this
performance is patently reflexive, as when in "Leaves" the voice
describes a blue jay on a twig outside his window—"Momentarily
sturdy, he stands astraddle, his dingy rump toward me, his head
alertly frozen in silhouette." A few sentences later, after the bird has
left, he notes that "there, a few lines above, he still is 'astraddle,'

his rump 'dingy,' his head 'alertly frozen.'" Reflexive, "deconstructive" even, this fiction bears out the abstract-personal mode by withdrawing from, moving away from the immediate particular as sufficient unto itself. One thinks of Wallace Stevens' (some lines of whose provide the epigraph to *The Music School*) first dictum to his long poem *Notes Toward a Supreme Fiction*, "It Must be Abstract." And Harold Bloom directs me to Valéry's dictum that "It is necessary to abstract oneself from the spells of life and from immediate enjoyment, even if for this purpose we must make a stern effort against ourselves."

As with Stevens, withdrawal from the particular in the interests of deeper authority and comprehension doesn't mean an absence of particularity in the sentences. Quite the opposite, since one only moves toward authority and comprehension by saying one thing in terms of another, again and yet again, as does the insomniac man in "The Dark" who finds that it isn't dark but something else: "visitations of positive light that were hurled, unannounced, through the windows by the headlights of automobiles pausing and passing outside." How to comprehend these visitations except by strenuous verbal play, by extreme metaphoricity (as current jargon has it):

> Some were slits, erect as sentinels standing guard before beginning to slide, helplessly, across a corner, diagonally warping, up onto the ceiling, accelerating, and away. Others were yellowish rectangles, scored with panes, windows themselves, but watery, streaked, the mullions dissolved, as if the apparition silently posed on a blank interior wall were being in some manner lashed from without by a golden hurricane.

The prose's strenuosities perform the man's restless registerings of the light. Whitney Balliett's marveling, at the beginning of Updike's career, at the writer's "sixth sense" is borne out by such prose, which is even more aggressive, on the move and insatiable, than in earlier stories from *The Same Door* and *Pigeon Feathers*. This is part of what I mean by Updike Experimenting.

38

Updike in Cincinnati

Robert Frost once famously said about poetry that "The whole thing is performance and prowess and feats of association," and he wondered why critics didn't talk about those things. The reason is that it's easier to talk about some stabilized meaning or significance that can be extracted from the volatile poem or story and ironed out into orderly critical prose. In Frost's and in Updike's cases, this saves the critic from having to come to grips with the feats of association as the work unrolls, a process in which meanings are made and unmade and the ground is always shifting, sometimes falling out from under us. In Updike's performance, as in Frost's, the feats are inseparable from the exciting, sometimes unsettling, shifts of voice that carry us along. This is why classroom "teaching" of the literary performance must centrally involve reading aloud, by way of suggesting the aural energies of the piece in question. Updike's experimenting, in these *Music School* short stories, involves more daring shifts of voice than in most of his previous work, and these happenings are crucial to the life of the story. In the remainder of this talk, I propose to concentrate on my personal favorite from *The Music School,* "Harv Is Plowing Now," in order to bring out some of that life.

IT IS A STORY of eight pages, divided into three more or less equal parts. Sketching them very broadly: part one begins, "Our lives submit to archeology," then moves into a memory of the narrator as sick child, huddled by his parents into blankets and warmed by an old stove in their Pennsylvania farmhouse. It then directs us to a neighboring farmhouse inhabited by a woman and her son Harvey, who, hitched to his mule, plows the land every spring. The second part develops the archeology metaphor, first by telling a story about the excavators of Sumerian Ur, then personalizing things by comparing the narrator's own stratified existence and examining the absence there of a once-present woman. In the final part we are transported to a beach at night, a poignant conversation with the woman who was once there, and some concluding metaphysical and ultimate reflections by the man. Like the other

39

Elliston Room Panel

"experimental" stories in *The Music School,* "Harv Is Plowing Now" is about loss, guilt, and the attempt at recuperation through the weave of words and sentences.

What is the most useful, most faithful way for a critic writing about the story, or in a classroom "teaching it," to behave? My sense is that commentary must resist the impulse to be too complete, too finished; it must be a little—to use Susan Sontag's phrase—"against interpretation," the better to suggest and pay respect to the consciousness of the story as it unfolds itself. For this reason we should regard somewhat warily criticism that, however informed and thoughtful, overdomesticates the literature it would explicate. As one who has written about Updike, I could find examples of such domestication from my own words, but for safety's sake I take the following sentences from Robert Luscher's very professional and informed study of the short fiction. He says about "Harv Is Plowing Now,"

> [It] links art and archeology as it depicts the narrator's medi-
> tative descent through the layers of his past: his present
> cluttered single existence; a bygone relationship that seems
> willfully buried and oddly barren; and, at bottom, memories
> of his rural childhood existence that focus on the image of
> his neighbor Harv, plowing the fields in spring. Although the
> base layer of his memories harks back to a pastoral realm
> much like Olinger, the narrator does not retreat to his hal-
> cyon past but rather discovers in it metaphors with which to
> begin the process of recovery that eludes other bereaved
> characters.

True, but not true enough as far as should concern a reader of the story. For what this orderly summarizing prose leaves out is everything that makes the experience of reading the story exciting. "Power ceases in the instant of repose; it resides in the moment of transition from a past to a new state, in the shooting of a gulf, in the darting to an aim," writes Emerson in "Self-Reliance." I should say the power of this story has ceased in the repose of the critic's sentences, since the transitions are what is left out.

How to describe the power of transition in Updike? It must involve, surely, matters of aural performance, the shifts and surprises we experience as one voice succeeds another. In the story's opening:

> Our lives submit to archeology. For a period in my life which seems longer ago than it was, I lived in a farmhouse that lacked electricity and central heating.

Here an authoritative, remote, knowing, philosophical voice is followed, without explanation, by a retrospective, autobiographical, "personal" one. To be sure, the terms of the comparison, the metaphor, will declare themselves as we move along, but it's at our peril if we lose the surprise, the momentary confusion, the sense of something glimpsed before it can be properly named and classified, that is the literary performance. In Frost's words from "The Figure a Poem Makes," "No tears in the writer, no tears in the reader. No surprise in the writer, no surprise in the reader." Like the related stories in *The Music School,* "Harv Is Plowing Now" takes its inception from tears in the writer, from troubles that the artful weave of sentences assuages but doesn't expunge. Critical commentary must somehow take account of that.

Although Harv himself, featured in the story's title, is long gone to Florida, the memory of his plowing the fields each spring is, in Mr. Luscher's reading, "a metaphor for preparing the soil of one's soul, tilling all the layers to ready the ground for new growth." But in the actual weave of the sentences he is both more and less than that, as the narrator remembers him "fat but silent footed," standing outside the parents' house with uncocked shotgun and beagles. It is the sound he makes that captivates:

> He preferred to talk outdoors, and his voice was faint and far, like wind caught in a bottle; when at night he hunted coons in our woods, which merged with his, the yapping of his beagles seemed to be escorting a silent spirit that traveled through the trees as resistlessly as the moon overhead traveled through the clouds.

A truly Wordsworthian figure Harv has become, not a man at all but—like the idiot boy or the leech gatherer—an extraordinary mythic presence, somehow blessed with a deeper life than is granted ordinary lives. And of course that life is the life of poetry, as evinced by the sentences just quoted that figure him as wind, spirit, the moon, and the clouds—as Nature. The image of Harv plowing, beautifully done, "repainting the parched pallor of the winter-faded land with the wet dark color of loam," is another more-than-human touch: "It seemed to be happening *in me,*" says the voice, italicizing the mystery. But that mystery is enacting itself in the sentences as they succeed one another, in the changing metaphors, the elusive poetry that make up Harv.

For me the most mysterious and elusive moment in the story comes in its second part, after the archeological account of the excavators of Ur and the levels of civilization they discovered. As the narrator moves into the stratifications of his own existence, he finds at the top "a skin of rubbish," quotidian life; at the bottom is Harv, eternally plowing:

> Between them, as thick as the distance from the grass to the clouds and no more like clay than fire is like air, interposes the dense vacancy where like an inundation the woman came and went.

The voice raises itself to underline a point to its listener:

> Let us be quite clear. She is not there. But she *was* there: proof of this may be discerned in the curious hollowness of virtually every piece of debris examined in the course of scavenging the days.

The more he goes on trying to be "clear," the more confusing and entangling is the prose, as it finds each fragment "hollow *in the same way;* and a kind of shape, or at least a tendency of motion which if we could imagine it continuing uninterrupted would produce a shape, might be hypothesized." The emphatic italicizations, the insistence on being "quite clear," create an expressive voice of anxiety, of "trouble," given body in the dense layering of figurative activity going on, the effect of which is to make things anything *but* "clear."

This is writing that doesn't want to be understood too easily; in fact, doesn't want to be "understood" in the manner of a more conventional story. The voice is always a little ahead of us—a little ahead of itself as it risks obscurity and clumsiness. It reminds me of Thoreau's first and last sentences of his paragraph in *Walden* in praise of "extravagance." It begins, "It is a ridiculous demand which England and America make, that you shall speak so that they can understand you," and concludes, "The volatile truth of our words should continually betray the inadequacy of the residual statement." An active reader must register such betrayings, and the narrator also seems to worry about them when, midway through the story, he retreats, or rises, to firmer ground, with the long catalogue of what's found in "the surface layer of days."

Who is this woman who *was* there but is not now? Donald Greiner, whose grasp of Updike's short fiction is unrivaled, says he is the narrator's divorced wife who shows up on the beach in the story's final section. I hold back from this identification for two reasons: first, in companion stories—"Leaves," "The Stare," "The Morning"—the lost woman, the woman who came and went, is a lover not a spouse. But more importantly, I think the writing takes her out of the spousal category—just as Harv is no mere plowboy—and makes her into something else. "Does the imagination dwell the most / Upon a woman won or woman lost?" asks Yeats in "The Tower." I should say that Updike's imagination dwells most upon the woman lost, substituting poetic figure for specifiable human identity. If this feels like a slippery argument, it seems to me a necessary one if we're to give credit to the strangeness of this stylistic art.

I have been attempting to suggest by way of illustrative example, the necessity (using another distinction of Frost's) to be an ear-reader rather than merely an eye-reader of Updike's sentences. A final example is the story's conclusion:

On the beach at night, it is never totally dark or totally silent. The sea soliloquizes, the moon broods, its glitter pattering in hyphens on the water. And something else is happening, something like the aftermath of a plucked string. What? Having fallen through the void where the woman was, I still live; I move, and pause, and listen, and know. Standing on the slope of sand, I know what is happening across the meadow, on the far side of the line where water and air maintain their elemental truce. Harv is plowing now.

I've always found this sequence extremely moving, and in thinking for this occasion about why, would locate that effect not in anything our narrator "knows" that he didn't before, but in the power of the transitions to the paragraph: transitions from poetic sensitivity ("The sea soliloquizes") to the interrogation of what is happening ("What?") to bold affirmation and repetitive grandeur ("I move, and pause, and listen, and know . . . I know what is happening across the meadow"), to the final utterance, delivered in a toneless voice beyond the nameable range of expressive choices and possibilities. "Harv is plowing now." In "The Short Story and I," Updike wrote that "Stories, with their falsified names and ambiguous conclusions, their hovering 'weave,' convey most closely human experience within my ken, in my time." To confute one of Updike's early critics who claimed that he had nothing to say, here, in the hovering weave of this ambiguous conclusion, Updike has everything to say, and the reader is correspondingly rewarded.

John Updike, Don DeLillo, and the Baseball Story as Myth

DONALD J. GREINER

My subject today is baseball, but I must begin with a confession. Standing before you in the heart of Cincinnati Reds country, I confess to being a long-time Cleveland Indians fan. I ask your forgiveness.

I want to focus on Mr. Updike's story about Ted Williams, titled "Hub Fans Bid Kid Adieu," and on Mr. DeLillo's story about Andy Pafko and Bobby Thomson, titled "Pafko at the Wall," and its subsequent appearance as the prologue to Mr. DeLillo's novel *Underworld*. I call your attention to two epigraphs that establish the frame for my remarks. The first epigraph is by Mr. Updike: "Baseball is a game of the long season, of relentless and gradual averaging-out" ("Hub Fans Bid Kid Adieu"). The second epigraph is by Mr. DeLillo: "Longing on a large scale is what makes history" (*Underworld*).

Midway through the twentieth century, the United States created a decade known today as the fifties. Emerging first from the debacle of the Great Depression and then from the terror of World War II, America stood preeminent, with its economy flourishing and its cities intact. An implacable enemy may have lurked across the ocean as a Cold War took shape, but a victorious nation exhausted by twenty years of economic depression and violent death required renewal rather than confrontation. It is not that Korea, McCarthyism, and racial tensions were ignored but that a generation born into debt and weaned on warfare sought rejuvenation.

From the perspective of today, the fifties look eerily innocent despite the unsettling tremors of cultural imperfection. This is because the decade offered a moment for the society to recharge its myths, to reaffirm the stories that point to its sense of its own identity. Don DeLillo and John Updike acknowledge this imperative, and they do so through two now legendary baseball games that began and ended the fifties and that, in the succeeding years, have achieved the power of myth. DeLillo's recreation in "Pafko at the Wall" of the third playoff game between the New York Giants and the Brooklyn Dodgers on October 3, 1951, the game in which Bobby Thomson hit a home run in the bottom of the ninth inning to lift the all-but-beaten Giants to the pennant, brilliantly captures a moment at the beginning of the decade when a nation elevated an apparently insignificant sporting event to the heroic in its need to counter the startling news that the Soviets had on the very same day exploded a nuclear device. Updike's account in "Hub

Fans Bid Kid Adieu" of Ted Williams's last game on September 28, 1960, the game in which Williams hit a home run in the final plate appearance of his long career, freezes a moment when the hero encounters the twilight and the fifties stumble to a close. Both writers recognize the power of language as an arbiter of history.

There are two important textual states of DeLillo's account of Bobby Thomson's home run: the short story "Pafko at the Wall" (*Harper's,* October 1992) and the novel *Underworld* (1997). After revising the magazine story to prepare it as the prologue to the novel, DeLillo published in the *New York Times Magazine* an account of the genesis of the tale titled "The Power of History," in which he argues the authority of language to counter the triumph of death. Just as Updike will note the ephemeral quality of *Saturday Evening Post* cover drawings in his story about Ted Williams's final game, so DeLillo begins his article by commenting on the transitory nature of newspaper reports.

The front page of the *New York Times* for October 4, 1951, published the day after Thomson's feat, carried juxtaposed headlines in identical typeface: "Giants Capture Pennant" and "Soviets Explode Atomic Bomb." DeLillo felt the power of history in the pairing of the home run known as "The Shot Heard 'Round the World" and the Soviet mushroom cloud. Yet the point here is not the startling, parallel headlines but DeLillo's decision to "be objective in the face of something revealed, an unexpected connection, a symmetry." The key word "connection" and variations on it turn out to be the operative thematics in the short story that became the prologue to *Underworld*. Rather than stress the potential of the bomb (politics) to dwarf the magic of the home run (myth), he acknowledges the juxtaposition and then celebrates the social connection that the Giants-Dodgers game affirmed. Updike would agree with DeLillo that "a fiction writer feels the nearly palpable lure of large events and it can make him want to enter the narrative."

DeLillo locates "a precious integrity in the documents of an earlier decade" that counters today's frenzied craving for time to move faster. He and Updike slow down the craving by freezing a moment of unexpected heroics and connecting it to history. Describing, for example, the archival newsreel footage of Thomson's home run, DeLillo notes the union between an isolated moment at the beginning of the fifties and the changelessness of art: "But the shakier and fuzzier the picture, the more it lays a claim to permanence. And the voice of the announcer, Russ Hodges, who did the rapturous radio account of the game's final moments, is beautifully isolated in time. . . . Thomson and Hodges are unconsumed." They are unconsumed because they enter the realm of legend, because they answer humanity's need for assurance, continuity, heroism, life.

DeLillo may imagine J. Edgar Hoover as counterpoint to Thomson's exploit, but his larger concern is that language itself carries the power of "counterhistory." Both history and fiction are narratives, but the latter connects humanity to sustaining myth: "It is fiction's role to imagine deeply, to follow obscure urges into unreliable regions of experience. . . . Such qualities will sooner or later state their adversarial relationship with history. . . . Language lives in everything it touches and can be an agent of redemption." This is where DeLillo and Updike soar, where they challenge history's (and Hoover's) "triumph of death," where they sustain us with a fixed moment of myth located in the artistic use of language.

In this deeply felt essay, DeLillo pointedly announces his understanding of his story. History is always infiltrated by the novelist's art, by what DeLillo defines as "the tendency of the language to work in opposition to the enormous technology of war that dominated the era and shaped the book's themes. The writer sets his pleasure, his eros, his creative delight in language and his sense of self-preservation against the vast and uniform Death that history tends to fashion as its most enduring work." Language can be artistic, sustaining, necessary. It connects rather than separates, affirms rather than denies. Fiction, concludes DeLillo, is "our second chance."

Rather than name the prologue to *Underworld* with the title of the short story, "Pafko at the Wall," DeLillo revises to use the title of Bruegel's famous sixteenth-century painting "The Triumph of Death," a print of which J. Edgar Hoover examines while ostensibly watching the playoff game. Two other revisions are relevant in the change from short story to novel: (1) DeLillo toned down the racial theme, but (2) he enhanced the emphasis on myth by altering the final word of the story from "now" to "past." For DeLillo, the green spaciousness of the stadium at the Polo Grounds suggests an immediate counter to the blackness of World War II, and the baseball teams themselves are the social glue of a culture. Although there are thousands of empty seats (thus uncannily presaging the thousands of no-shows at Ted Williams's last game at the end of the fifties), Russ Hodges understands that the game connects to the past in a historical continuity of heroic achievement: "Polo Grounds—a name he loves, a precious echo of things and times before the century went to war."

Sitting together in the stands, Frank Sinatra, Jackie Gleason, Toots Shor, and Hoover personify the opposite perspective. They are Bruegel's skeletons dancing on the backs of the living. Hoover focuses on the blast of the Soviet bomb because he yearns to link the fifties to the deaths in World War II and to the specter of Communism, but DeLillo and the fans focus on the blast from Thomson's bat because they sense the connecting authority of myth. Stories that join a culture give it the will to resist death.

DeLillo makes the contrast explicit. Here is Hoover, brooding in the stands, longing but failing to join the anonymous fans: "He wants to feel a compatriot's nearness and affinity. All these people formed by language and climate and popular songs. . . . But there is that side of him, that part of him that depends on the strength of the enemy." Now, here is Hodges, musing in the broadcast booth: "a souvenir baseball, a priceless thing somehow, a thing that seems to recapitulate the whole history of the game every time it is thrown or hit or touched."

DeLillo and Updike affirm a society's need for faith, for what the former calls "magic" and the latter calls "miracle." To believe is to hope and to hope is to live. It is not that they are ahistorical, or that the bomb did not explode, or that McCarthyism did not exist, but that a nation turning toward Bruegel and Hoover rather than toward the legends created by Thomson and Williams is a nation depleting itself. Late in the game, for example, with the Giants on the edge of defeat, the crowd unifies in rhythmic applause, and "the repeated three-beat has the force of some abject faith, a desperate kind of will toward magic and accident."

DeLillo's irony, on the other hand, reduces Hoover to a merchant of death. As the magazine pages with the reproduction of Bruegel's painting flutter onto his shoulders, "It is clear to Edgar that the page is from Life [magazine]." To parry Hoover's commitment to death in life, DeLillo posits Thomson's home run as a feat of strength and skill that both mythologizes a moment in history and forges a unity among the living. Not only do "people make it a point to register the time"; they "wish to be connected to the event. . . . This is the nature of Thomson's homer. It makes people want to be in the streets, joined with others."

The decade of the fifties ended with a similar moment of magic. On 28 September 1960 John Updike bought a ticket to Fenway Park in Boston to watch Ted Williams play what would turn out to be his final game. Updike's account of that legendary contest, titled "Hub Fans Bid Kid Adieu," has been praised as consistently as any of his short stories, for it extends the genre of the short story by deliberately blurring the line between essay and fiction. "Hub Fans" is a short story cast as an essay. Like most of the chapters in Mr. Updike's collection of stories about sports titled *Golf Dreams*, "Hub Fans" is one of his many variations on the standard form of the genre. This is because he not only includes the documented facts of baseball history but also recreates himself as a key character who muses on both the mythic home run and his own reaction to it. Indeed, I call "Hub Fans" a lyrical meditation, closer to, say, "When Everyone Was Pregnant" than to "A & P."

Like DeLillo's recreation of the Thomson home run, "Hub Fans" has multiple important states. The story was first published in the *New Yorker* (October 22, 1960) without explanatory footnotes. Updike then added the notes to the second state when he collected "Hub Fans" in *Assorted Prose* (1965). Then, in 1977, he published the third state of the story in a limited edition of 326 signed copies (Lord John Press), for which he wrote a four-page preface.

The context in which Updike created his lyrical meditation on heroism is set not by the contemporaneous *Rabbit, Run* (1960) but by a little-discussed short story, "Packed Dirt, Churchgoing, a Dying Cat, a Traded Car," which he published in the *New Yorker* (December 16, 1961) before collecting it in *Pigeon Feathers* (1962). In this story the narrator responds to a sailor's question about why he bothers to write: "We in America need ceremonies, is I suppose, sailor, the point of what I have written." "Packed Dirt" and "Hub Fans" appeared little more than a year apart, at a time just before the disasters of the sixties sullied the American glow first emanating from victory in World War II and then sustaining the nation through the undercurrent of death fed by the twin demons of McCarthyism and the Cold War.

Just as DeLillo researched the specifics of the Giants-Dodgers game in back issues of the *New York Times* and in Hodges's recorded play-by-play account, so Updike resorted to an "outdated" record book and the Boston newspapers. His goal was not an expository reconstruction of the event but a meditative exploration of the moment. Played on a dreary, chilly New England afternoon, the game turned into an unanticipated ceremony of mythic proportions which, when looked at retrospectively, seemed to bring the fifties to a close.

Updike's description of Fenway Park cleverly presages the paradoxes of the man he will laud in the story. Fenway offers "a compromise between Man's Euclidean determinations and Nature's beguiling irregularities." Like Ted Williams, not to mention American society itself, Fenway Park is far from perfect in its oddities and twists. And yet it is also the locale of heroic action, "a lyric little bandbox of a ballpark." Updike plays on the contrast between the irregular and the precise throughout the story, juxtaposing the gray day, the thousands of empty seats, and the meaningless game against the Baltimore Orioles with the life-affirming green of the stadium, the presence of Ted Williams, and the fans' longing for a miracle from the aging hero.

By the third paragraph, however, it is clear that the fans linked together on this cold afternoon represent Americans needing rejuvenation at the end of a spent decade. They have come to see the greatest hitter of the era, and they recognize the potential for ceremony in the event: "The affair between Boston and Ted Williams was no mere summer romance; it was a marriage composed of spats, mutual disappointments, and, toward the end, a mellowing hoard of shared memories. It fell into three stages, which may be termed Youth, Maturity, and Age; or Thesis, Antithesis, and Synthesis; or Jason, Achilles, and Nestor."

On this particular day at Fenway, Updike's Ted Williams becomes god, hero, and artist for reasons beyond his career-long prowess with the bat. Playing in a game that means nothing since the Boston Red Sox are mired in next-to-last place, Williams is the fifties's last best hope for heroism. What was "magic" for DeLillo turns into Updike's "miracle": "All baseball fans believe in miracles; the question is, how *many* do you believe in? . . . It was for our last look that ten thousand of us had come." Updike challenges the saccharine portrayal of the national essence dispensed in the fifties' mass media via Norman Rockwell's magazine covers: "Whenever Williams appeared at the plate . . . it was like having a familiar Leonardo appear in a shuffle of *Saturday Evening Post* covers." The reader of DeLillo and Updike can hardly fail to notice the parallel dismissals of *Life* and the *Post* as shapers of American culture.

Fittingly for those who enter myth, Williams rallies the populace as he walks to the plate for his final at bat in his final game. The dreary day, the boring contest, the washed-out decade—all

Elliston Room Panel

point to the triumph of death. Yet Updike and DeLillo celebrate the creativity of language and power of art: "Understand that we were a crowd of rational people. . . . Nevertheless, there will always lurk, around the corner in a pocket of our knowledge of the odds, an indefensible hope, and this was one of the times . . . when a density of expectation hangs in the air and plucks an event out of the future." Williams swings, and the ball, "less an object in flight than the tip of a towering, motionless construct . . . , was in the books while it was still in the sky." Never vainglorious, never playing to the crowd, always committed to his art, Williams circles the bases, refuses to lift his cap to the imploring fans crying "to be saved," and steps into the permanence of legend: "[I]mmortality is nontransferable. The papers said that the other players, and even the umpires on the field, begged him to come out and acknowledge us in some way, but he refused. Gods do not answer letters." DeLillo and Updike know this truth. Yet they also know they can shape language to memorialize the exploits of the gods that connect a society in the face of diminishment and loss. Myth counters death.

In the years since its original publication, "Hub Fans Bid Kid Adieu" has achieved a special status. For example, David Halberstam includes the story in *The Best American Sports Writing of the Century* (1999). Even more significant was Williams's response to Updike's story of his heroics. In the preface to the 1977 limited edition of "Hub Fans," Updike reports that Williams, through an agent, invited Updike to write his biography. The invitation was declined. Yet Updike uses the preface to confirm the longevity of myth. Gods may not answer letters, but now, years after the miracle, Updike is pleased that true gods remain aloof. Unlike "some former superstars," Williams "does not appear on Brut television commercials or in Marilyn Monroe biographies." The allusions to Willie Mays and Joe DiMaggio are barely hidden.

Like DeLillo, Updike does not doubt that art shores up a culture or that a culture needs ceremonies. Thus, at the close of the preface, he shifts from the message to the means; from the heroics described to the description of heroics; to, in other words, the language: "Love shows. Readers sense, an inch or so under the words, love or its absence, . . . so these paragraphs must be, or they would not have survived their occasion."

The point is clear. Mythic feats and artistic language outlive the political turmoil of their times. John Updike and Don DeLillo confirm that a society is finally sustained by the stories it remembers to tell.

Response

JOHN UPDIKE

Unlike these two academic types, I do not have a paper prepared. I thought I would share with you what occurred to me as I listened to these two papers. A writer is of limited critical usefulness in regard to his own work. The only thing he can bring to it is his memory of the writing of it—what was on his mind, and what he hoped to achieve. Let me begin with Bill's very eloquent and, as always, shrewd and yet affectionate and responsive paper. I think that among critics Bill is very special in his tolerance for a variety of writers and forms, and the basic hopefulness with which he approaches a page of prose or poetry. I was very grateful that he deemed me worthy of a book-length meditation.

On this whole matter of critics, it is true enough that Henry Bech relished the death of one of his tormentors, enough so that he then embarked upon an increasingly purposive campaign to kill a number of his worst critics. And so in our minds we would eliminate them if we could. One of the disadvantages of even the most respectful and positive résumés of our careers, such as Professor Pritchard's book, is that of necessity the critic "on your side" has to quote, often in extenso, those critics who were not on your side. So adverse reviews or notices—whether by Harold Bloom or Frederick Crews or John Aldridge or a woman called

Rabinowitz years ago—that you had hoped would fall into the abyss of time that Don DeLillo so movingly evokes in fact have this terrible afterlife of being quoted again and again. The same quotes recur. "He has nothing to say," which was said of the book called *Of the Farm,* written when I was almost a child. But it's become a kind of epitaph on my career. So that any criticism has the painful quality of collecting again these burrs that your woolly socks have picked up and there's no getting rid of. There's no end to these burrs, they are ever with you; no doubt above my deathbed some well-wisher will quote Harold Bloom, who said stingingly that I would never, never, for all of a bunch of virtues that he listed rather hastily, attain the American sublime. Don DeLillo is very much interested in the American sublime, of course. I've never quite thought of it that way, as something you could attain to, although I'm rather pro-American, as writers go.

Let me talk a little bit about "Harv Is Plowing Now." I just reread it for the first time in many years and I was astonished I had the nerve to write it and that the *New Yorker* in that far-off era printed it, because it borders on incoherence. It was one of a series of stories, which Bill has already described or alluded to, stories of assemblage; the compound title, "Packed Dirt, Churchgoing, a Dying Cat, a Traded Car" really united four story ideas or near-ideas that I couldn't see individually carrying the freight of a narrative. But put together they seemed to elaborate the same theme. So, too, a compound story called—what is it called?—"The Something Man of Boston"?

JAMES SCHIFF

"The Blessed Man of Boston."

PANEL [MORE OR LESS IN UNISON]

"The Blessed Man of Boston, My Grandmother's Thimble, and Fanning Island."

UPDIKE

That's right, I have all of these Updike experts here. It makes me feel relatively ill informed. Again, these stories, these fragments are very disparate. One about the loss of my grandmother's thimble, leading to a reminiscence about my dear grandmother, mingled with the glimpse of a man seated in Fenway Park, a big Chinese man. I think in that benighted era we even called them Chinamen. While the rest of us were filing out, he was still sitting in the stands with a serene aura about him; like a pebble left after the tide is moving out, there he sat. There was the notion that all of existence is at some level ecstatic, and that he was experiencing the ecstasy. This theme of mine, again and again I return to it—the quotidian, the daily, the ordinary which is, at some level, I don't want to say sublime, but it's ecstatic. Anyway, this combined with the lost relative (more than a relative, really, because I lived with my grandmother for my first twenty-four years), plus Fanning Island, a haunting image of an island in the Pacific. Let me just tell you, now that I brought it up—I didn't mean to talk about this at all—Fanning Island is a small island in the Pacific where people have found various artifacts indicating life, remnants of huts and so on, but the people who created and used the artifacts and shelters have vanished. And how so? How could they? The theory is that, of course, a canoe of all men washed up on this island and the men lived out their lives, but without women there was no subsequent generation. They died out, one by one. And this is a haunting embodiment of Pascal's image that we are all like creatures sitting in a prison watching other people get their throats cut; one by one we're pulled out of a cell and our throats are cut. So it's about death, as are many of my stories.

"Harv Is Plowing Now" is again a set of fragments, three things that don't seem to have much to do with each other but which, in some way, seemed to me to cohere around a basic lump of loss, sorrow, and grief,

which I was feeling in the era of the six stories that Bill mentioned earlier. Behind them, more or less clearly, is an affair which the narrator
has had with a woman he has loved and lost. And, of course, as Yeats
so well put it in his epigrammatic way, a woman lost is more interesting than a woman not lost. So around this ache, this story was con-
structed sentence by sentence, and I think that fiction in that time of
my life served me as a kind of therapy. Just putting things down and
trying to make shapely paragraphs assuaged my sense of a dislocated
life, and of a dreadful mistake having somehow occurred.

"Leaves," I think, is the first embodiment of this feeling and maybe
the purest. At least from the ardor with which I apparently defended it,
and still defend it. I think it's really a beautiful story written in a kind
of trance of misery. Written very quickly, but every sentence did feel
very secure. And it's about in some way trying to elevate the personal
erotic misadventure with an existential sense of the strangeness and
basic tragedy of our mortal existence. The theme of archaeology, of our
lives as strata down through which we can delve, recurs in my work. A
rather recent story, "Personal Archaeology," appeared in the *New Yorker*
last year, and again there's this notion that we are the topmost layer of
a whole layer of selves that lie beneath us. I've always been interested in
archaeology; all this information about Ur and Harappa came out of a
book by a certain Leonard Woolley that I read years ago.

There was a blessed time in my life when I could read what I pleased
and what interested me, instead of books that friends had written or that
I was supposed to review. And in that wonderful period of free-ranging
reading I used to buy little Pelican books, a lovely blue border around
them, full of information about this and that. I remember I bought one
and read it called *The Badger,* so for a time at least I knew much of what
was to be known about the badger, a theme that didn't resonate with
me quite the way Ur had. The eight feet of solid clay represents a flood,
an inundation that the narrator feels is analogous to the period in his life

when he was in love with the woman, the woman who is now gone and who does indeed reappear, at the beach, in the flesh. But in the flesh she is dismissive and defensive and unmythic, you could say. She's just a woman trying to pick up the pieces of her life, and the last thing she needs is to be approached by a former lover with a need to round things out or to elicit reassurance.

I was struck, rereading it, by the fullness with which I evoked the old farmhouse and my being sick. We think back so nostalgically to periods of sickness, we seem more intensely alive somehow, when children—that wonderful feeling where you don't have to go to school. Your parents bring you food periodically, and you can listen to the radio as much as you want. My mother used to make me cinnamon toast, which was buttered bread sprinkled with cinnamon, cut into three strips, and brought to me as a reward for being sick. It's not the only reward but it was an authentic one and one that I remember. Anyway, that first miserable winter we moved to the farm I was sick, and the coal stove seemed to be my only defense.

"Harv Is Plowing Now." What is the story about? Well, we all have our approaches and the critics are welcome to theirs. But it seemed to me it was about renewal. That Harv in the spring is plowing is one symbol of renewal, of the world beginning again. The narrator's dismissal by the love of his life, as he construes her, still leaves him standing, still leaves him alive under the stars and he, too, is free to begin. [reads from story] "[T]he stars seem to me a roof, the roof of days from which we fall each night and survive, a miracle." Again, "The Blessed Man of Boston." Life, existence is a miracle. [reads from story] "[S]urvive, a miracle. I await resurrection." Meaning not so much life after death, but life after love. That there is more life to be lived, of the quotidian kind, described in terms of the very scrambled artifacts he finds when digging down through the quotidian days that were interrupted by, as did use to happen in suburbia, an affair. "Tears"—a lovely quote of Frost—Tears, yes there has to be a sorrow. My generation, having been raised on Eliotic criticism and the magical phrase "objective correlative," had the faith that if you, the writer, have enough tears and are feeling something strongly enough, almost anything you put down will serve as an objective correlative for the emotion. I expected somehow that if I put down what was on top of my mind, the sense of sorrow and loss and slow renewal would come through. And, apparently, the *New Yorker* agreed because they took the story and published it.

Let me say, lastly, about short stories and criticism that a critic has to assume that the author had a tremendous array of choices, of sentences, words he could have chosen. You could have written these words and not those words; another sentence could have followed this instead of the one that did. But, in fact, to the writer doing it, what you turn out is more or less what you can't help turning out, and this is all you *can* turn out. So that it's not as if you have very many choices at all, and what seems to be a pondered device is really just the author's own helpless voice. We all talk in a certain way, and writers write in a certain way.

Certain themes recur. The theme of the daily, I was struck by that. My one commercially successful, you could say, novel, called *Couples*, was originally going to be called *Couples and Houses and Days*, because life, as I felt it and was trying to describe it, was about not just couples but about the houses they lived in. The fascination exerted by other people's houses; the notion that more happiness is happening in those houses than in your own; the look, in a small town, of other people's lit windows and the imagined bliss and contentment transpiring behind them as you drive by. And then of course the days, the days that keep delivering sunrises to us and then sunsets, and that seem, in their long parade, to bring us some treasure which we persistently misreceive. So that even in a novel like *Gertrude and Claudius*, which takes place in medieval Denmark, supposedly, Gertrude sits there thinking about the days, how they differ, how her life is made up of these days, these days.

We are told, "Seize the day," and basically we do and don't. We seize it in some sort, but often seem to have missed the essence.

As to Don's lovely and appreciative meditation on the Williams piece, what can I say? I went to the game kind of by accident. There was something else I might have done that day in Boston, but it fell through. It was a different world in 1960, and things were much less hyped than they are now—and they were probably more hyped in 1960 than they had been in 1920. Although it was Williams's last day and he had been *the* dominant sports figure in New England since his arrival in '39 or '40 with the Red Sox, there were close to twenty thousand empty seats. It was, of course, a gray day and a meaningless game in the league standings. Nevertheless, I was surprised that more people hadn't shown up to see what was certainly going to be Williams's last day of playing in Boston.

Don spoke about the mythmaking capacity of sport, but the appeal and reason that we're all to some degree sports fans is that sports events are stories that are occurring as you watch, that are being created as you watch. There is *no* way, except for very dishonest and rare fixing, and maybe professional wrestling—there is no way to script the end of a sports event, so that these two home runs that DeLillo and I wrote about were by no means foreordained. A home run is still hard to hit, a feat. To that extent, these are antistories. Or they are "really real" stories in that they are happening, like our lives, every minute as we watch, and they unravel in real time in the way no work of fiction can.

I have written very little about sports or baseball. I was not so much a baseball fan as a Williams fan. In Pennsylvania, in the forties, I fell in love with Williams basically as a set of numbers. A friend of mine had a game in which you spun a dial, and as each player came to the plate you put on the dial a card, which accurately reflected the player's batting statistics. And here was this Williams, who had better figures than DiMaggio. So suddenly there was this mythic person—who was this bland-sounding Williams? Then when he returned from World War II I was able to follow him and that first marvelous Red Sox postwar team, the '46 team that should have won the World Series easily and failed to—the first of the Red Sox failures which have inspired so much verbiage in New England. My goodness, how they go on and on about the Red Sox, as though most teams in most leagues don't lose every year. That's why we care. The winners are rare.

But I had followed him intently. I had a lot of information in my head; the myth had been formed in my head. The Jason/Achilles/Nestor analogy had occurred to me, or was easily there for me, so it's not as if I had to research it—I did have a beat-up old fact book that I consulted. The *New Yorker* in those days did not run baseball stories. Harold Ross was a man of many prejudices, some of them unspeakable, but a speakable one was that he did not like baseball. And though he ran columns on boxing and track—those of you who are of an age can remember that there was a thin column about track, not running but horse racing, which appeared every week—so that miles and miles were printed on horse racing and nothing on baseball. I was delighted that William Shawn, who had replaced Ross as editor, took the piece.

It was a story that wrote itself for me. I couldn't have written it without Williams hitting the dramatic home run the way he did. What I was hearing in Don's recapitulation of the account, what sticks in my mind from that day, is the way I found myself moved, standing in the eighth inning when Williams came out for what was surely the last time in Boston. Everybody, instead of cheering, stood and applauded in this semisilent wave of applause, like after a symphony or something. On and on, on and on, the sense of the years unrolling. This region had for twenty years been wed to this man, in a sense, and had shared the disappointments of Williams's career, the well-known ten games in which he did not hit even a mere .250. So it was like some of my short stories, an exercise in nostalgia. These sports figures become vessels wherein our lives are contained, as they develop histories that intertwine with our own personal histories, so that perhaps that's what makes them worth thinking about, or worth loving. They may not be lovable in themselves. Williams was a very prickly fellow. DiMaggio, it turns out, was not very nice. And Babe Ruth; even in his lifetime it was known he had many deplorable character qualities. But we loved them, given the very finite and, in a way, ridiculously specific challenge of hitting a rapidly moving ball, because they rise to the occasion; they do their best and that's why we love them. We store their feats and their feats become part of our lives.

Maybe I've said more than enough. I'm appreciative of both these learned men taking the trouble to meditate upon my work, which is composed really in a rather desperate fashion, which doesn't anticipate academic study. It's a little like a sports event, in that you show up on the field and hope something nice happens, but you're never sure it will. It's torn from the fabric of your own life, often in what seems a perilous and even illicit way. But you're hoping to make out of the rubbish, the quotidian rubbish of your own life, a few objects that will somehow be worth examining and treasuring, as in archaeology, later. Thank you.

SCHIFF

We have a few minutes and can take some questions.

AUDIENCE

One of the great charms of rereading some of your fiction lately has been to look at stories at different times and to notice how much, even as a very young writer, you were in love with the feeling of nostalgia. It colors so many of your early stories. *Pigeon Feathers* is bathed in a kind of nostalgic light, even though you were thirtyish when you were writing that. I wonder if you would care to comment on the way that nostalgia has a certain value for you, as a kind of move toward experience or maybe away from experience, that has served you so well through your career.

UPDIKE

This room is small enough that you all heard that question, didn't you? Related to my long-term fondness for nostalgia, or the nostalgic quality of my work from early on. You don't have to be very old to be nostalgic. I mean, you can find a fifteen-year-old boy discussing himself when he was eight with great nostalgia. When we're youngish we have rather recently discovered ourselves as creatures in time, with a past—it's when we first realize that we have a past, in fact—and certain things we've experienced now become joined with the past, this majestic lost-ness and pastness of history that DeLillo evokes with his home run, and much of the subsequent novel.

One day I woke up, and I was thirteen, and World War II was over. It was over. I had never, in a way, imagined it would ever be over because it had dominated that particular early adolescence/late childhood of my life. To know that all sorts of artifacts go with it, of course: all of the little flags that people with soldiers in the home in service hung in their windows, all the rationing tokens, war stamps, V-mail, blackouts, air-raid drills. There was a whole world of wartime that vanished, and so it goes.

Now I find that the Cold War is over and has been over, and it is a little hard for me to adjust to a post–Cold War world. It seems relatively pointless to be an American. What's the point of being an American if we don't oppose the Ruskies? The whole sense of American virtue and specialness, in a way, flowed out of the fact that whatever faults we had, we were not Red, we were not Commies.

Fiction, like music, takes place in time and must deal with time and with the way time is always news to us. Something in us, as Tolstoy said toward the end of his life, is timeless, and we're constantly startled to

62

Updike in Cincinnati

find ourselves aging, to find certain people that we knew and loved are gone for good; so it's very natural, I think, that nostalgia is a great motivator of fiction. Even now at sixty-nine, I find the past, instead of becoming less vivid, has become more vivid. The wish to unearth it, in the sense of writing about it, does not weaken. Unless you have, I find, some sense of personal revelation that you might make public, and useful thereby, it's very hard to get going writing. It's this feeling of bringing this buried treasure to light that keeps you excited.

AUDIENCE

I think you're very modest about your achievement in writing, talking about how the writer just kind of extends himself and that's what we see. Especially in these stories that Bill is talking about: the lyric, the abstract, the personal. And the comment you just made, I thought, was very instructive: fiction takes place in time. But it seems to me in these stories that somehow you are transcending that by moving through the music of imagery rather than narrative time. Would you care to comment on that paradox?

UPDIKE

Is it a paradox? The companion story to "Harv Is Plowing Now" is a story called "The Music School," which is similarly assembled of disparate bits, mixing deep past and present, and is much more spiritual or religious than the first-named story. It begins, "My name is Alfred Schweigen and I exist in time." Silence and music both take place in time; in fact silence, in the form of rests, is part of music, as well as the background of it. So it was on my mind that music flows in time and lives do too. What the artist hopes to do is to freeze time by writing something that will last, and to fix a passing moment with phraseology that will make it memorable and eternal, or what we think is eternal, but, of course, is not eternal but a somewhat lasting life in print. We all

Elliston Room Panel

have artistic impulses as children and we're all, to some extent, drawn to the permanence, the apparent permanence of art. Your parents save your drawings; you can beat the doom of time by means of art. I was fortunate in that I've been allowed to extend this fantasy into my adult life and to become a professional artist. So that all I can say about my imagery is that I'm trying to stop time in a way, and give myself more time than my seven score and ten. Three score and ten. Would it *were* seven score and ten. Yes?

Some prizes are given to heroes who deserve them, who ought to be immortal, timeless. In the city of Cincinnati, I think I can say, I'm a visitor, that Pete Rose deserves to be in the Hall of Fame. And I think you deserve the Nobel Prize for literature. Would you care to comment on that analogy?

UPDIKE

Well, I suspect the forces preventing Pete Rose from being in the Hall of Fame aren't quite the same that keep me from winning the Nobel Prize. But there may be a similar taint attached to both of us. Certainly on the statistics, baseball is a game of statistics, and Pete's statistics are Hall of Fame quality, nobody would argue with that, nobody does argue. But baseball also has been established in the American psyche as a moral exercise and an epitome of American virtue. And when, after the Black Sox scandal of 1919, which seemed to bring the game down to the level of pool-hall sharks and fixed horse races, it took a highly moralistic commissioner, Judge Kenesaw Mountain Landis, to restore an appearance of virtue to baseball.

Nobody deserves the Hall of Fame, statistically, more than Pete Rose, unless it would be Shoeless Joe Jackson, who is kept out of the Hall of Fame by the same, in a way, hypocritical establishment. He was tainted.

Updike in Cincinnati

Shoeless Joe, who was possibly the greatest natural hitter who ever stepped up to the plate, was denied as well. I would think that eventually Pete Rose will get in. I don't know if we'll ever see Shoeless Joe Jackson get in. What do you think—you baseball experts around me? [muffled no's from panel] No? It's a tragedy of a sort. A jury, by the way, found him and his seven teammates not guilty of throwing the 1919 World Series.

WILLIAM PRITCHARD

Yeah, but what about the Nobel Prize?

UPDIKE

I think I would not mind seeing Shoeless Joe Jackson get the Nobel Prize. He qualified about as well as some of the recent winners. No, actually, the Committee does a good job. I mean, you think of being sixteen Swedes sitting up there trying to sort out world literature and distribute the honor equally. It's a tough job. I wouldn't want it.

AUDIENCE

Kind of a quotidian question. It's about coming up with titles for short stories. It's hard to do. And they seem to come in bunches. You have some strung together titles. I was interested in the title last night of "Snow Falling in Greenwich Village" and then something like "Leaves." How do you decide? Do you have a method, any patterns that you've been able to discern? Do you try a whole lot before you settle on one?

UPDIKE

Some stories are harder to title than others. The name of that story, by the way, was "Snowing in Greenwich Village." Although maybe it should be "Snow Falling on Cedars" instead of "Snowing in Greenwich Village." I was very much taken at that time with an English writer called

Henry Green, whose titles were mostly gerunds: *Loving, Living, Party Going.* I thought that was a good light-handed way. It has a hint in it of life, this being an ongoing process; life is gerundive instead of a matter of past participles.

Usually I have the title before I begin. I say usually, maybe 60 percent of the time. Sometimes, indeed, the title is what gets you excited enough to begin. Some stories languish for want of a title. A story called "Flight," which I always thought was one of my better stories, was called "First Flight" initially, and I forget when the "First" was dropped. But it was, and it's better without it. Shorter is usually better. It's nice to bestow a title that people can remember. So for that reason a simple title is to be preferred to a complex or long one, although long titles also have their vogues. Raymond Carver was fond of long titles, and I noticed a story by Ann Beattie in the *New Yorker* that was called "That Last Odd Day in LA." Some of Salinger's titles are quite nicely long. I think it's more important to have a good first sentence. A first sentence that arouses suspense, and a last sentence that, in some way, lets you feel that the story is over, that this particular curve of action has been described. But I haven't really answered your question. I think the title must in some way amuse the writer. If it amuses the writer, it's more apt to amuse the reader than if it doesn't.

AUDIENCE

Could you comment on your writing and editing process, and how that's changed over the years as you sit down to write?

UPDIKE

Reflecting on the writing process, it hasn't really changed an awful lot. I still try to write something each day, and my quota used to be three pages or three hours. It doesn't usually take three hours to write three pages, but sometimes it takes you three hours to get settled. There's more and more extraneous stuff to do in my life; I find it's harder to get to the real writing. But it also might be that I am, as my wife has suggested, more ingenious at thinking of methods of procrastination. The older I become, the more distracting junk and invitations that arrive in the mail. But for any would-be writer, I advise a daily habit of writing something, even if it is relatively modest.

Henry Green, whom I mentioned before, had for much of his career, even the best part of his writing career, a full-time office job managing a good-sized English firm. So he could not write during the day, and would come home at night and, as he described it, have a drink and sit and try to write a page. I don't think the drink was a terribly good idea, though it didn't seem to hurt his quality till the end; he did become an alcoholic ghost of himself, and stopped writing. But up to then, he wrote nine wonderful novels and a memoir, I think all fairly slowly. It's odd that your mind is able to remember what you're doing amid the thousand topics that your brain has to entertain, that it's able to pick up and advance a written narrative a little further. But it's the same thing with reading a book: amidst all that's crammed into our head, we're able to keep the thread of the book we're reading. The brain is really a marvelous organ in its capacity to store and sort data. Like a language: a language can seem to be lost in there, but you go to the country where it's spoken and it comes back.

AUDIENCE

I know your mother was a writer. Could you talk a little about her influence on you?

UPDIKE

It's hard to separate her influence as a writer on me from her influence as a mother. But watching her write was one of the things that made me feel this was a feasible activity. There weren't too many examples of

Elliston Room Panel

writers in the Berks County of my boyhood, although it was a middle-class world that believed in books. Your piano teacher would have the latest John Steinbeck on her shelves behind the piano. It was a world where books were a common coin of cultural currency in a way that I'm not sure they are now. I mean, you go into very well-furnished houses that seem to have no books in them at all; that was less true in the thirties and forties, I think. My mother cared about words; not only her stories but her letters were chiseled and well phrased, and her devotion to the written word probably did descend to me.

Of all the examples your parents are trying to set for you, of course, your first reaction is to wind up doing the contrary. I did not begin as a would-be writer. I liked to draw; the payoff is quick for a child, and the models of drawing are all around you in comic books and so on, pictures on the walls. It was only rather slowly, at college, that my center of gravity shifted from drawing into writing. And, of course, then it began to pay; I began to get published, and to get money for it, so it became irresistible to me. You can also draw in words in a way you can't cartoon. I think the attempts to make comic strips literate—*Maus 1* and *Maus 2,* and a few other brave experiments like that—tend for me to fall kind of flat. There are limits to pictorial narrative, whereas there is almost no limit to verbal narrative. You can do any crazy thing in it that you have the power to do.

AUDIENCE

What kind of critical response did you receive for *Licks of Love* and "Rabbit Remembered"?

UPDIKE

Licks of Love got mostly good reviews here. There was one very sour review in a Los Angeles paper, very negative; the reviewer said that "Rabbit Remembered" was just unrelieved banality. And, of course, it is meant to be unrelieved ordinary life in a way. My attempt in all the Rabbit books, to some extent, is to make banal, ordinary, otherwise lost life interesting enough to read about; and you're going to fail with some people. You have to assume a certain level of patience and interest in readers. The English reviews have been a little more sort of "show me" in their attitude. The English have this notion that I am a towering establishment figure; at the same time, they find what I'm describing quite alien and odd. So they're more willing to pay abstract homage than actually to settle in with the books and try to figure it out.

Michiko Kakutani, every writer's friend, didn't much like the twelve short stories; she thought they were tired. And of course I do know that these are kind of wrap-up stories in a way; I wouldn't call them dregs, but they're plainly reaching down into territories where I've been before. But she did like the Rabbit novella; she read it with a good spirit and got sort of with it, which I guess is what you hope for from critics—that they drop their own preconceptions of what a book or narrative should do and kind of get with yours. I find, as a reviewer, that if I like a book I tend to write the review in somewhat the style of the book. I mean, I've been infected, to a degree, by the book.

SCHIFF

Just one more question.

AUDIENCE

In *Gertrude and Claudius,* part of King Hamlet's tragic downfall or flaw seems to be that he's taken the divine right of kings too much to heart, and I was wondering if you see any way for Christian society to accept this sort of kingly office, but not through being a king?

UPDIKE

In my somewhat fanciful prequel to *Hamlet,* King Hamlet, who appears in *Hamlet* itself as a ghost only, is a man who takes being a king seriously. He's worked his way up the ladder. He married the princess of the reigning king, and one of his instruments of rule is the church, as it existed in medieval Scandinavia. How sincere is his Christianity? I think quite, actually. One of the things Gertrude doesn't like about him, down deep in her own Viking nature, is his piety. She likes Claudius because he's rakish and irreverent, and she dislikes her husband because he is pious and obsessed with responsibilities of his office.

On the general topic of the divine right of kings, Shakespeare wrote frequently. He seemed to take the view that, good or bad, a king was a king, and that a sin inhered in disobeying or slaying even a bad king, that there was something divine in the office. Many societies have governed themselves through this principle, though it's led them into a lot of demented and inefficient and corrupt monarchs. One thinks of Turkey as an example: those Ottoman sultans who got increasingly demented, and were demented in part because the ruling sultan would imprison his brothers in solitary confinement, where they had almost no contact with any other man and their only contact was really with the harem. They would emerge after forty years in captivity with no social skills; and these men were expected to rule. This is an extreme example of the potential ineffectiveness of inherited kingship. I would not recommend that America revert to it, but it is an ancient institution that elicits a deep human response. We are, in effect, inviting God to rule us through this appointed person on earth. It is a system that works better in theory than practice.

SCHIFF

Thank you, John. Thank you, Bill and Don. And thanks to everyone for coming out this morning.

Updike in Cincinnati

Cincinnati Art Museum: Updike viewing *A Venetian Woman,* by John Singer Sargent

Cincinnati Art Museum

Cincinnati Art Museum: Updike examining *Eve Hearing the Voice*,
bronze sculpture by Moses J. Ezekiel

Cincinnati Art Museum: John Updike and museum Director Timothy Rub
beside the bronze sculpture of *Model for the Tyler Davidson Fountain,*
by August von Kreling

Elliston Room: *left to right,* Donald Greiner, James Schiff, John Updike

Elliston Room

Elliston Room: *left to right,* John Updike, William Pritchard

Elliston Room

A Conversation at the College Conservatory of Music

Wednesday, April 18, 2001, at 2:00 p.m.

Werner Recital Hall

Campus interview before an audience of two hundred

JAMES SCHIFF

John Updike is no stranger to interviews. In his career he has submitted to many, and he has written, particularly in his short fiction, about being interviewed. In the final story in *Bech at Bay,* Henry Bech, who has just received the Nobel Prize in literature, rants against having to appear on TV talk shows while his publicist tells him how wonderful he was on *The Charlie Rose Show.* To which Bech replies, "*Charlie* was wonderful. I hardly said a word." Shortly thereafter we see him on *The Diane Rehm Show,* and a caller asks if, indeed, it was true, "as she had read in the *National Enquirer,* that Mr. Bech had recently fathered a baby out of a young lady a third of his age?" Finally, in his story "One More Interview,"

Updike's actor-protagonist exclaims, "I can't stand interviews!"—but by story's end he's demanding that his interviewer write down every single detail and name that the actor can recall from his childhood. With these fictional episodes in mind, I will push forward, albeit cautiously, with this afternoon's interview.

My hope today is that we can, at least in part, cover some new territory by focusing on the short story. John Updike has published more than two hundred short stories, and his stories have been chosen for inclusion in *The Best American Short Stories* and *The O. Henry Prize Stories* on at least twenty-five occasions. It may be difficult, as I said this morning, to find an American short-story writer in the last hundred years who has been honored more often. In addition, while the timing of this festival has not been ideal in regard to local events, it could not be better in regard to recent developments in John Updike's work. Last year he edited the massive *Best American Short Stories of the Century,* and in the last six months he has published two short-story collections, *Licks of Love* and *The Complete Henry Bech.* Whereas John Updike's alter ego, Henry Bech, is a writer of low output—to the extent the American Academy presents him with the Melville Medal, "awarded every five years to that American author who has maintained the most meaningful silence"—Mr. Updike himself is a very busy and productive writer who, in his thirteen collections of short fiction, has given us some of America's finest stories. Good afternoon, John, and thank you for being here.

JOHN UPDIKE

Not at all. It's a pleasure to be here.

SCHIFF

I wonder if we can begin by going back to Plowville, to the sandstone farmhouse which you've written so eloquently about and where you spent your adolescence. Your mother had her own literary ambitions, and as a child and teen you watched her type her stories and mail them off to magazines in hopes of publication. What exactly did you make of what your mother was doing?

UPDIKE

Well, I did watch. From a child's point of view, I can remember a moment in the front room in the house in Shillington, which is where I lived until I was thirteen, when I was sick in bed and had a lot to say to my mother, and she finally indicated—she was at her desk trying to write—that she wanted me to be quiet. I was an only child, and much indulged, and I'd never before been asked to be quiet, so I realized this was a very momentous activity she was engaged in.

I don't know exactly the curve of her ambition or her life. As with many a dead parent, there are many questions I'd like to ask her. I should have thought of them at the time. Like me, she was an only child, born in 1904 in a community called Plowville (though that wasn't the legal address). Where this lonely farm girl got the idea of becoming a writer I've no idea. I do know that she went to Ursinus College outside of Philadelphia, where she met my father. She was always the baby of her class. She had been skipped through the one-room country school and went off to normal school at the age of twelve, which she always said was too young; those four years remained painful in her mind. At sixteen, she went off to Ursinus College, and again she was the baby of her class. She graduated at the age of twenty and took a year of graduate study at Cornell. A professor called Lane Cooper, I believe, encouraged her somewhat in her ambitions. She did get a master's degree, married my father a few years later, and worked at various odd jobs. At some point she moved back home with her parents. They wound up all out of work, thanks to the Depression, and it was into this household that I was born in 1932.

A Conversation at the College Conservatory of Music

Her ambitions to write existed in Shillington. I can remember a novel she wrote called *Twelve Days*. I was invited as a child, as a sympathetic child, to read these things, so at about the age of eight I became one of the youngest unpaid editors in the country. And I do remember that *Twelve Days* took twelve days out of a woman's life and told her life in terms of these days, which always struck me as an interesting idea. But when she died at the age of eighty-five and left quite a few papers, I could not find this novel among them.

She had the ambitions of most writers of that time. She wanted to be like John Steinbeck and John Marquand and the other dignified but popular writers who appeared in the magazines and appeared on the bestseller lists and sent off stories to *Collier's* and the *Post*, which was only fifty miles away, of course, from our part of eastern Pennsylvania. *Liberty*, *Cosmopolitan*, I guess, *Redbook* certainly—they always came back, sometimes with a little encouragement written on the rejection slip. She was one of those writers who was frustratingly close to being publishable. And I could feel, even as a child, the closeness, and I didn't have it in me to boost her over that perilous edge into print.

But when we moved to the country in '45 she renewed her efforts. It wasn't easy living in a very small house with her son, her husband, and her parents. But she had it in her heart to write about Ponce de Leon, who was the Spanish conquistador who first set foot on Florida. Really, he was the first European since the Vikings to set foot on the mainland of North America. For that brief moment in the history of the world, Florida was America. My mother wrote her novel in the first person and that didn't work; it came back from the New York publisher. So she wrote it in the third person. And time goes by—I went to college, I began to get published, she became middle-aged, her parents died, and in the vacuum created by her—this is more than you wanted to know, Jim and audience, but it's a storyteller's instinct to give you the full thing. In the vacuum left by her parents' death, she actually, for the first time, had a little time and money to do some research; she took three trips to Spain to search out the sites at which Ponce de Leon would have been a page and a courtier in the court of Queen Isabella. First she went with an old college roommate; then with my father, and he died not too long after. I wouldn't say that the trip killed him, but it didn't make him any better, certainly. And she had a chance to use her little Spanish that she had acquired by explaining to a waiter who was trying to serve the two of them—"Es enfermo," he is sick. So literary research can help with real life. I took the third trip with her, I and my daughter.

She never was able to quite make this novel work. It was a lesson for me: a writer should know when to quit on a project. But, on the other hand, I've had a thing about James Buchanan, a very different kind of historical figure, but one who has fascinated me; you get to feel that there is something here only you can tell about this historical figure, which leads you to devote a lot of time to what may seem to others to be futile. What I got from my mother, as the first writer I ever knew, was the devotion it takes and the solitude of the craft. Because you are alone and you want to be alone, you don't want your child prattling at you.

And her love of words, her love of the right word. We had not a very large library, but we did have some books that she cherished. I used to go at her side to the Reading Public Library in the nearby city of Reading and have an experience of books en masse; these towering walls of books in the forties made an impression on me. To think of being one of those authors seemed to me like being an angel in heaven. This was a kind of heaven, a heaven of permanence, a heaven aloof from the eddies and floes of material life. So her ambition to write seeped down to me, and I was the lucky one who became a writer first. But, to end this story on an up note, she did get published in her fifties. The *New Yorker,* still capacious and embracing of new talent, took about ten of her stories. So her story is not an unhappy one, but she was a struggling, as they say, writer. And when I get letters from other struggling writers, I remember my mother and think of how little a word from the world of the published means to the vaster world of the unpublished.

There were interesting moments, I imagine, during that time in which you, your mother, and your son were all being published simultaneously in the *New Yorker*. What was that like?

UPDIKE

That was a strange and happy confluence there. My older son and second child, David, was born in 1957 and attended Harvard, Class of '79, exactly twenty-five years after my class of 1954. He had not shown much literary interest as a child. I rarely caught him reading a book; it was a very different kind of upbringing than I had had. Television had come to exist, and television was always there in the home as something you could turn on. Furthermore, he had three siblings and I had had none. So there was every reason for me to read and for him not to read. He was attracted to a young would-be writer at Harvard, and I think it was partly a courtship maneuver when he himself began to write. I was pretty young when the *New Yorker* took my first story; I was just out of college and twenty-two. But I think David might have been twenty-one when they took a story of his. It was a beautiful, happy story, like the first story my mother had accepted. Her story was about her grandfather's death and was probably the best thing she ever wrote. David's was about a dog who accompanied him in his boyish rounds around our place in Ipswich, Massachusetts, and at the climax of the story he looks down and sees that the dog's muzzle is gray and realizes that the dog has grown old. It's a wonderful moment, and I'm not sure if I'm doing it full justice.

But, yes, David began as a writer kind of at the top, and he sold the *New Yorker* as many stories maybe as my mother did, perhaps ten. But

76

Updike in Cincinnati

tastes change, editors change, and he's not had many acceptances lately. But he still is, at the age of forty-four, working at being a writer. And, yes, it was strange having all of us appearing in print in the same magazine. I felt like the middle of a sandwich. I was the ham in a writer sandwich.

SCHIFF

You published your first short story as well as your first poem in the *New Yorker* when you were twenty-two. But you had been publishing locally a good deal before that, first in the Shillington High School *Chatterbox* and then in the *Harvard Lampoon*. During your four years with the *Chatterbox,* you published, I believe, 285 poems, articles, reviews, and drawings. In addition, at age fourteen you wrote a rather sophisticated murder mystery that stretched to perhaps 70 manuscript pages. What was fueling that drive? Was it simply the joy of putting words together, or was it getting into print, or was it saying something new?

UPDIKE

I'd never counted those *Chatterbox* pieces, but they were generally very short. There was a lot of light verse. I think the first kind of writing that I felt compelled to emulate was light verse as it was practiced in the forties and thirties by—Ogden Nash is the first name that comes to mind, but there was also Phyllis McGinley and Arthur Guiterman and E. B. White and Morris Bishop. There was a whole host of writers of light verse, some of whom appeared in the *New Yorker,* others in New York newspapers when there were more newspapers and when newspapers had more space to devote to literary activity. So light verse was kind of everywhere, and I was a would-be cartoonist; my first ambition was to make funny drawings, and it's not such a great step from that to try to make funny poems. It was on the strength of that slight ability I developed, plus my cartooning, that got me onto the *Lampoon,* at Harvard, where I did write and draw a lot. These undergraduate publications have the great advantage, for a would-be writer, of needing material. It's the opposite of the real world, where there's too much material. Many issues of the *Lampoon* I wrote at least half the content, not because I was worthy but because I was willing.

Jim, you're asking basically why was I so willing, what fueled this burst of adolescent and postadolescent wordsmithing? I think it's probably inadequacy in other realms that led me to look for salvation in being published. I was afraid of the process of time; I was afraid of death, of being—I think Unamuno somewhere said—eternally forgotten. And being published in whatever form is some kind of a safeguard against being eternally forgotten. So there is a religious bliss, of a sort, that attaches to print, and there also is an aesthetic bliss.

My first publications were mimeographed. The *Chatterbox* was mimeographed—most of you don't know what a mimeograph machine is, of course. That shows how old, in truth, I am. But you cut a blue stencil, it was a sheet of delicate wax, and if you cut it or typed onto it, it made white on blue, and then a rotating drum, inked, would press through the white lines and make ink on the outside. And that was the way the *Chatterbox* was published, both drawings and typed material.

Harvard, though, offered me the bliss of real type, hard type, in those years set by Linotype. And your drawings were turned into metal "cuts," out of copper alloy. Talk about permanence! To see a drawing that you had done out of your head on paper with ink, and to see it turned into metal, and if you asked, to be able to keep the metal, was a wonderful kind of purchase on lastingness. So I've always had this concept of writing as a transitional process, something on the way to getting into print. The payoff is print. And the notion of writing for the pleasure of it, or as a letter to your grandchildren or anything more abstract than getting published, isn't very real to me. In this way I'm something of a crass throwback to another era. I meet young writers now who don't care, they tell me, if they get published or not—the bliss is doing it, expressing yourself is enough. For me, no, I needed the confirmation of being part of an artifact that could be distributed in the economy and would, in some small way, perpetuate your identity in places where you'd never been, and eventually into decades where you wouldn't be alive.

SCHIFF

Turning to the short story, are there factors, besides length, that distinguish the short story from the novel? Are there different strategies, different attitudes toward character and toward delivery of your narrative?

UPDIKE

You don't always know if an idea is a short story or a novel. *Couples* was first a short story, but when I wrote it out as about a forty-page short story it seemed very crowded. Clearly this was a theme, the theme of interrelated couples that, if you're going to tackle it at all, needed space, the kind of space a novel could provide. And, in fact, *Couples* was not even a short novel. So there was a case of a slight misstep. I'm trying to think of a novel that should have been a short story; I'm less good at that. There probably were some, but in general a short story presents itself to you in much the way a poem does: the idea makes the small hairs on the back of your neck stand up, as Housman wrote about poetry. It's something either in your own experience or in other people's experience. The short-story inspiration can come from a variety of places, some near and some far, but it's something that seems worth packaging. It's definitely a packaging problem, and you think of it, indeed, as an item of a certain size. You might be a little wrong about the size, but you can certainly tell the difference between a ten-page story and a thirty-page story. Thirty pages is almost the outer limit for me of what I consider to be a short story.

Not to be too workshoppy about it, but it's a single idea, a single motion often in a continuous time span, carried forward, like a kind of gesture. Now there are short stories—one thinks about Alice Munro—which have more directional arrows in them than this. And, indeed, even I've written some that are not especially simple, but, by and large, you have a vision of a topic, a character, a landscape. I've written stories about family reunions, written stories about an anonymous person worrying about death while having insomnia, as well as more traditional stories of he said/she said. Nevertheless, you have to have the beginning or you can't begin, and you should have the ending, I would say, so you know where you're headed and to give the reader, when he or she is done, the sense of having read something *intended*, something shaped.

You're sometimes wrong. The story "A&P," which many of you may have at least flipped past in anthologies, originally went on. After Sammy resigns, in my conception of it, he went down to the beach to try to see these three girls on whose behalf he'd made this sacrifice of respectability, on whose behalf he'd broken with the bourgeois norm and let his parents down and Mr. Lengel down. And he doesn't see the girls, and the story ended somewhere there. But my editor, the recently deceased and very wise and gentle Bill Maxwell, and others—because with the *New Yorker,* as with most magazines, you don't get just a single editorial opinion; you talk to a single editor who often expresses the views of several editors—thought the story ended somewhat earlier, ended with the resignation. So there's a story I didn't perceive the ending correctly, but which worked out anyway.

A novel is rather more a field of ideas, a broader social topic. How can I say? Let's think of some novels. *Rabbit, Run* was written on the premise that there was a kind of American being produced in the world around me, in fifties America, who peaks with his athletic career in high school. America is full of people who would've liked to have stayed in high school but weren't allowed to. Maybe most of us are a bit like this. My father, who was a high school teacher, would bring home tales of this and that former athletic hero who'd fallen on hard times, drink and divorce and all the sins horrifying to good Lutherans like us. And for some reason in the middle of Ipswich, Massachusetts, three hundred miles from the place of my birth, at the age of twenty-seven, I decided to try to tell the story of such an ex-basketball player, such a former hero.

It seemed to me there was something worth telling about it. It was a piece of Americana that was not fully revealed, although others, such as William Inge in the play *Picnic,* have touched upon this fact of American life. It valorizes the qualities of youth, and at the same time it gives us medicine in which to live on and on, and what do we do with this long rump of our lives that we're stuck with? The novel also says something about freedom, because Rabbit has experienced bliss of a kind, and he's imbued with the American notion of freedom. At what point does the exercise of your own freedom begin to extract too high a price from others? We are members of a society, as well as free religious units; and so on.

Couples works from the thought that in the early sixties, in the absence of competitive claims from other institutions, young married couples were making institutions of each other. And that friendship and the interaction of suburban couples, the interaction which begins generally over the children who create the friendship and extends into games and parties and a daily closeness that comes to include sex but is really more than that and that is a relief from the tedium and the boredom of monogamy—in all this, extra-monogamous circles are created which in some ways are like churches. So that I guess what I'm saying is that a novel demands more characters and a fuller, more leisurely exploration of a given idea.

SCHIFF

You mentioned the Rabbit books and *Couples,* where there are so many more sociological references, historical allusions, and quotidian details

A Conversation at the College Conservatory of Music

than in your short fiction. The story, presumably, does not provide adequate space to expand in these ways. Is the short story, then, less contemporary, less temporal, more eternal perhaps? Also, in comparison to the novel, is the short story more or less autobiographical?

UPDIKE

The short story is often—I'll speak from my own experience—more directly autobiographical. It's rather hard to write a novel about a character who is very much like yourself. The lead character, and indeed all the characters to some extent, take life from your own. Rabbit and I share impulses and thoughts; the hero of *Toward the End of Time* and I share impulses and perceptions, but there has to be a difference somehow, a distance for the spark to jump. There has to be something different that entertains you to be in this other life, in this other head. You sit down to read because you want to enter lives other than your own, and you write, to some extent, for the same reason: you want to be in a life other than your own. So that my attempts to write directly out of my own experience at novel length have fallen short, whereas it can be done in a short story. You just don't need that distance to keep you amused for the course of a week. But there does have to be *something* in it that feels external and invented, and something that you imagine will be interesting to people who don't care about you and your problems.

That's one of the hard things for would-be writers to realize: you don't owe the reader an awful lot, but you do owe the reader an attempt to divorce the narrative from your own special pleading. Some stories feel like special pleading: the writer is begging for your forgiveness, or complicity, or some sort of personal alliance. No. None of that. Whatever your problems, you are, for the length of the short story, trying to make a document from which you can be forever detached. And this feeling of making discrete, often indiscreet but d-i-s-c-r-e-t-e, discrete verbal tales which have an interest in relation to the society, in relation to what you perceive to be human issues.

A central issue in *this* American writer's work is, of course, the question of where freedom ends. What do we owe other people? And equally, what do we owe ourselves? We're all intrinsically selfish. We're only given one ego, one life. To some extent our whole lives are just an attempt to take care of ourselves, and yet there also is a social contract out there which we unwittingly signed. So the tension, as it were, between the inner spirit, the infinitely appetitive and restless spirit, and the kind of compact we have to draw up with our circumstances continues to be a focus point of a lot of my stories. And I assume them to be part of the human condition, enough to interest other readers.

I don't know, Jim. It's very hard to describe. There's something about the short story; when the idea comes to you it just has a different color, a different size in your mind, as opposed to a novel. A novel you can foresee certain developments, and you know there will be awkward patches where you'll want to give the whole thing up. Whereas a short story will only be held within yourself long enough to be kind of breathed onto the page. It just happens. It happens fairly readily, in a week or two, say.

SCHIFF

Some have said that your work in short fiction has not been as experimental as it could be. They may be unaware, however, of the lyrical pieces in *The Music School* and the montage stories in *Pigeon Feathers*. I'm interested particularly in the montage stories, one of which is titled "Packed Dirt, Churchgoing, a Dying Cat, a Traded Car." Lorrie Moore says of that story, "I was stunned, held paralyzed by the story's beauty, as if by some genius Doberman pinscher. I could not move to read anything else. Surely I would never read anything else, ever, only this. I held the book so long, I got a paper cut and bled on the page." Can you discuss the genesis and development of that story? It did seem like you were doing something new, and I wonder whether you had any doubts about what you were attempting.

UPDIKE

Those are wonderful quotes from Lorrie Moore. To make Lorrie Moore bleed on the page is something to which I never dared aspire. How nice that she, who's a writer of such talent herself, would phrase this old reading experience in such generous terms. This is the kind of reaction you hope for but don't often get, or at least you don't get word of it that often.

I'm trying to remember the circumstances. I know that I wrote that story and the preceding one in a terrible funk. I was prey, at spots in my life, to terror—angst to the point that I felt paralyzed and that all of life seemed a really miserable charade on a supercloudy day in a kind of a cellar, the cellar of organic existence. And it always tied into my Lutheran heritage, and no doubt was a replication in me of Luther's own gloom and the black moods which eventually gave us Protestantism. That is, a religiously disposed person feeling doubt is worse off, feels lower, feels more frightened, feels more oppressed than a person who has never had religious aspiration or was not indoctrinated in any religious faith. As far as my own circumstances went, I had much to be grateful for. I had a delightful, bright, attractive wife; a nice house in the middle of a very nice town with a beach and sandy marshes; a circle of friends; four small children; and a career at the *New Yorker*—they liked me down there. I was able to support myself fairly easily in this New England town on New York money, money that came out of New York. So there was no external reason to be so low.

Out of this funk I began to piece together a story of incidents none of which on their own would have quite made a story, ending with my father's heart attack at the age of sixty-one. I was about twenty-nine, and drove to Pennsylvania, and he was so amusingly himself, so brave and good about the whole thing. At the hospital I saw my father lying in his pajamas in this bed and [laughs]—as I remember it, I forget what really happened as opposed to what I made happen in the story. But some Lutheran girl did come around to try to give him religious comfort, and instead of being cool to her or rebuffing her as most people might have done, he was friendly, to the extent that she was sort of startled and alarmed by his friendliness. And he said finally, "You better go on and visit others. Sick Lutherans are a dime a dozen." Anyway, witnessing his particular courage—because he, too, was a man prone to what he used to call "the blues"; he'd say, "I've got the blues. I have the blues," the depression of the would-be religious—I felt he was coping with death on my behalf. He was out there, thirty years ahead of me, greeting it, confronting it, and I drove back somewhat restored, at least in the short story. This is a long way from what you were asking.

To the general topic of experimental, could I have been more experimental? I was trying to sell stories to the *New Yorker,* but the *New Yorker,* especially after 1960 and the advent of Donald Barthelme, was more open to experimentation than I think they got credit for being. So often, more than once, I wrote a story that I thought was too way out for the *New Yorker,* and they snapped it up. So I can't blame the *New Yorker* for whatever seems to be cautious and conservative in my approach to the short story. Certain experimental devices just don't seem to me to be worth the trouble. Faulkner's time-chops. The Joycean device of doing away with quotation marks and having dashes in front of speech just seems to me confusing; you don't know when the person has stopped speaking, depriving yourself of the interplay between the quoted words and the adjectival qualifications of these words. You're denying yourself, in my book, a kind of music. Look at Henry Green's dialogue, for example.

But I was as experimental in trying to express the elusive truth as I could be. This is not just my problem. I think you set up shop as a storyteller, a story maker, a story seller, and it becomes your product, something you're going to live by, like shoes. At the same time everything modernist in you questions convention. Does life really break down into stories? Why should a story have a beginning, middle, and end? Isn't there something mechanical about arousing suspense, having a conflict, and then resolving the conflict twenty pages later? I mean, is this really an adequate commentary on the actual texture and structure of lived life? No, it would seem to me not. And there's a certain resistance, just as in twentieth-century American painting there accumulated this resistance to making things look like things, to painting realistically. It wasn't that the masterpieces of Western art hadn't been realistic and representational, but something about depiction of this kind began to rub devoted artists the wrong way. To make another mural of farmers reaping hay, to make another portrait of a society lady, to make another painting of a dog—all of this eventually seemed not worth doing and, in some deep, deep way, false. And so it is with my own stories. Though I've turned out between two and three hundred, many of them have functioned through a basic resistance to tidy stories, or stories that end with a moral. When I first heard Salinger's stories being read to me in the early fifties at college, I was thrilled because here was a man who saw the problem, that life was not an O. Henry story, it's not even a story by John O'Hara. A story is a kind of wandering thing that ends ambiguously. Its beauty is that of the unpredetermined, somehow. So Salinger was, for me, a kind of gateway into a new sort of short story. But I think a lot of so-called experimentation, in fact, has been done and done to death, and has ceased to deliver the salubrious shock that it was meant to deliver and did deliver originally.

SCHIFF

The piece we've been talking about, "Packed Dirt," is listed as a short story, yet some view it as a sort of meditation or essay. This morning

Don Greiner was talking about how "Hub Fans Bid Kid Adieu," a base-ball essay, reads like a short story. In some of your nonfiction collections, which are typically comprised of book reviews and essays, you include first-person pieces and narratives. What distinguishes the short story from the personal essay?

Yes, in my case, certainly, the short story becomes very close to being a personal essay. I figure that if I have a name in there that's not mine, though, it is enough of a remove, and I'm able to talk in my own voice. Something about the false name frees you up to fairly uninhibited description of yourself because you become a specimen of the human predicament. You become a specimen human being even while remaining personal. But to me, those personal-seeming essays—and maybe it's some quirk in my own brain cells—don't have much to do with me once I've written them. They're out there, they possess whatever narrative interest they have, and it doesn't matter anymore how close or far from my own circumstances the stories were.

Any piece of writing is an act of communication, an act of social interaction even, so that you are leading the reader on. You are teasing the reader, you are trying to startle the reader, you are trying to give the reader a reason to keep reading. And this is as true, really, of a book review as it is of a short story. So that a reportorial piece like "Hub Fans Bid Kid Adieu" draws on the same narrative impulse, the same impulse to engage an invisible other person. And it's this desire to engage that, I guess, invents narrative strategies and creates a kind of fictional form. In the case of "Hub Fans Bid Kid Adieu," as I said a couple of hours ago, it was Ted Williams and the day and the events that created the story. I went to that ball game with no intention of writing a story about it; it was very far from my mind. But it suddenly seemed imperative that the world have an account of this beyond what the Boston papers would say the next day. So I took it upon myself, without any blessing from William Shawn, to write an account of Ted Williams's last at bat, and the *New Yorker* did publish it, and, as Don Greiner said, the story has had some success in sports anthologies ever since. But it's really my only sports story. For a time, editors would think that since I'd written about Ted Williams I could write about Larry Bird equally well. But though I could admire Bird, I was miles from being involved in the need to step out of my fiction-writing shoes and into a sportswriter's.

SCHIFF

So nothing on Tiger Woods coming up?

UPDIKE

Tiger Woods can hardly be overpraised. He's amazing, but I feel that he has been very adequately covered by the press and was so from the beginning. Even before he became a professional, everyone had their eye on him. The amazing thing about Woods is that he's been able to live up to highly inflated expectations. In a way, he's exceeded even the most high-flown hype he got; he's better than that. But I need, as a writer, somebody who's a little out of the way. And Williams at that moment in his career was kind of out of the way, playing for a whatever—a fifth-place ball club—and an old ballplayer who had hung on for one more season. So, I didn't feel I was jumping into a crowded space when I took it upon myself to write about Ted in his twilight.

Let me say, in general, that I need always some feeling of bringing news where news has not been brought before. I attended Harvard College, a place that has attracted much attention from literary-minded graduates, and I've never wanted to write about it much for that very reason. One short story—"The Christian Roommates"—and parts of a novel, *Roger's Version,* are all. Others have covered the Harvard story. However, certain Pennsylvania boyhoods, suburban mischief—I've felt that these thing have not been overcovered and that there was some space left for me to say something new.

SCHIFF

What about the *New Yorker*? The relationship you have shared with the magazine for nearly half a century seems to have been mutually beneficial, and your stories obviously brought something new to the magazine: a more poetic style and, I think, a sensitivity to domestic middle-class life. But my question goes back to Lorrie Moore, who has spoken of the "gentility of the pre-Gottlieb *New Yorker*," in which, she said, "No body fluids, sounds, or smells were permitted in its pages." Now you've obviously been very frank about human beings in your longer fiction, particularly in the Rabbit novels. But I wonder, did you ever feel constrained, particularly in your short fiction, about what you could say in the *New Yorker*?

UPDIKE

Yes, in a word, I did. There was no ten commandments handed down to you saying, "Thou shalt not mention excrement," or any list. But there certainly was a felt sense, just in reading the fiction that was there, of what parts of middle-class life—and it was almost entirely middle-class life—that would describe what would go. I did have an itch to tell a little more about the physical facts of human existence, and I guess that's one of the reasons I wrote *Rabbit, Run* and a novel like *Couples*—because I was in my own house instead of in their house, and free to say what I wanted. For that reason, the novels are more personal to me, it might be, than the short stories. I can't blame anybody else for the limitations.

There was a kind of prudery which became archaic actually during Shawn's long rule as editor. Ross was himself not prudish as a person, but he was prudish as an editor. There were many things he did not

89

A Conversation at the College Conservatory of Music

think should be in the magazine; he saw the magazine as entering a middle-class home and he wanted something that the children of the household would not be threatened by. This from a man who ran some very raunchy Arno cartoons in the twenties and thirties, as if he didn't know quite what they were saying. He was a funny mixture of shrewd-ness and naïveté, but more worldly in his behavior than Shawn. Shawn was prudish in his outward demeanor as well as in his editorial policies. He didn't like violence, really, of any sort. To some extent I sympathize with that, as most of us go through life avoiding violence and, except-ing wartime or an unusual accident or mishap, don't have much expe-rience of it. So I think violence is a drug that must be used sparingly by a fiction writer. The whole aim of civilized life is to create nonviolent cir-cumstances, and the *New Yorker* story traditionally is concerned with the violence that's not acted out: emotional violence. It's about, in a way, the repression that goes with civilization.

I pressed, in my shy way, against the *New Yorker*'s boundaries of de-cency. A story called "Wife-Wooing"—it surprised me when they accepted it. And they did get some angry letters about it because it described a husband and wife; it was a husband's monologue about his wife, and sexual rejection, and the opposite, and so on. But it's true that as long as Shawn was there, there were certain four-letter words that did not get into the magazine. With Gottlieb and Tina Brown, who rather rel-ished four-letter words, and now with Remnick, four-letter words are fine, and I'm not convinced that it's made a great improvement in the quality of the fiction, oddly enough. I think it was prudish, yes, and un-necessary, but I also think that certain words, certain concepts, certain activities, perhaps, should be held in reserve so that they'll have some punch when they are used. Though of course I do now use four-letter words in the *New Yorker*. Yeah, I think they're part of the language and part of life and proscribing them was in a sense false. But it was an honorable kind of falsity. I don't think the *New Yorker* stories were, in essence, false to the texture of life as most people, as most of their readers lived it.

You recently served as editor of *The Best American Short Stories of the Century*. In that role you not only read a great many stories but had difficult choices to make as to what would and would not be included. I wonder, in terms of reading a century of short fiction, what kinds of things you learned or discovered about the evolution and development of the short story? Where are we at now? Why is the short story not getting anywhere near the attention of the novel?

Has it ever gotten the attention of the novel though? I wonder. I think lately I've seen more articles about the short story, or this and that hot new short-story writer. In a strange way, the teaching of creative writing in every college now has made all the graduates of these courses, who themselves have written short stories, more attuned to short-story masters. So that somebody like Raymond Carver was able to achieve an almost mythic stature in his own lifetime basically through being read in college workshops. Lorrie Moore, likewise, to a degree. So I think there is a lot of interest in the short story.

That anthology. I was glad I said I'd do it because it's the only best seller I've been associated with in some time. But the job I undertook was very hedged. If somebody came to me and said, "I want you to concoct an anthology of a century of American stories," I think I would have to say no, because the amount of potential labor is tremendous, almost infinite. You would have to read though the stories of the named masters and then go searching for all those who didn't quite achieve that sort of status. And you'd be reading hundreds upon hundreds. No, my assignment was to pick the best of what had already been singled out as the best in various *Best American Short Stories* printed by, in recent years, Houghton Mifflin. I forget who published it in the first years, but anyway, it's a series that's been running since 1915 in which between twenty and thirty stories, considered the best of the year, are published. Not only did I only have to be acquainted with those, I didn't have to sift them myself. Katrina Kenison, who's been editing . . . what happens when you're an editor—do you care to find out how this works?

SCHIFF

Sure, sure.

UPDIKE

Katrina Kenison, who lives in Winchester, Massachusetts, and works with Houghton Mifflin in Boston, Massachusetts, subscribes to virtually every magazine that prints short fiction. She's a rapid reader and a conscientious woman and, out of this mammoth amount of annual reading, she picks one hundred short stories which she forwards to the editor, who is usually a writer of some repute. Out of that batch—maybe it's one hundred and twenty, but it's a very finite number—he or she picks twenty. Now you can have editors like John Gardner, the late John Gardner, who said, "No, I hate all these. These are dreary, well-written stories, and not my taste at all." So he turned to stories that he knew about, often as it happened of students he had taught, and so produced a kind of maverick anthology, which was within his rights as editor. But, by and large, most of us are more docile than that and take Katrina Kenison's word for it that these are, if not *the,* at least among the best short stories of the year. So I, in a sense, just did the same thing, only on a bigger scale.

I went through, I don't know, a couple hundred stories which she had pulled out of the earlier volumes. Some of which are very hard, by the way, to find. The ones in the teens and twenties were off most libraries' shelves; they ceased to be checked out and so were chucked. But she did manage to get a complete set together, and submitted her choices to me. My thought, when I undertook the assignment, was that this would be an opportunity to create an anthology reflecting the American short story in this century, at least since 1915. Already it's fudgy. There's no O. Henry, no Henry James offered in this selection because '15 was the cutoff year instead of '00. I figured there had to be a Faulkner, a Hemingway, a Fitzgerald, a Welty, a Katherine Anne Porter, and a Flannery O'Connor. There were maybe fifteen or twenty writers whom I was determined to include, and I did. I picked the best of the array I was given. As it happened, John O'Hara and Mary McCarthy had never made a *Best*. There was a very minor Salinger, and no Grace Paley. A lot of writers, of course, had been selected more than once, and made Katrina Kenison's distillation more than once. By the way, Jim, you've twice said today that you think I have more stories in these anthologies than anybody, but I'm sure that Joyce Carol Oates has more than I. Joyce Carol Oates is in almost every one of these books. It's a rare year's "best" that doesn't have an Oates in it.

SCHIFF

She does have more in *The Best American,* but I wasn't sure about the *The O. Henry Prize Stories.*

SCHIFF

Oh really? Maybe I've beaten her out? Did I beat Joyce Carol Oates out at something?

SCHIFF

We'll check the stats later. [Updike was correct. Oates has had more short stories in both series.]

A Conversation at the College Conservatory of Music

So my job was pretty easy, as these things go. I intended to include the writers I mentioned, and read everything else for the odd story that really touched me or rang a bell. There was a story by Elizabeth Bishop, the poetess, which just knocked me out. You read about three or four of these a night in bed, and you know, it's hard, if you're emotionally timid, to read many stories which are trying to shake you up, right? They are trying to unnerve you, to shock you, to run you through the catharsis process. And so I had trouble sleeping. Bishop's story struck me as horrifying and beautiful. It was about a pair of boys in Canada who were sent by their farm family out to guard the expensive farm machinery during a very cold spell, and they couldn't find the blankets that the hired man had left somewhere in the barn. So they curled up together in the straw and froze to death. A wonderful, ghastly story told in her poet's cool, meticulous voice.

I looked for stories out of the mainstream and picked a couple by authors who were totally nameless and had written almost nothing else. I wanted to produce some sense, to wind this up, of American life as it had changed since 1915. You had to have some stories that reflected the Depression, some stories that had a feeling of the Roaring Twenties, and so on. It was oddly hard to find stories that dealt with World War II. This heroic enterprise, which involved the entire country, nevertheless made a rather small dent on fiction. And the stories that Ms. Kenison did dig up for me were—what were they?—I wouldn't say mechanical but slightly predictable and slick. I wound up with a story by Hemingway's third wife, Martha Gellhorn. I hadn't thought of her as a short-story writer, but this story really did capture that slightly tired, frenzied feeling of the home front in World War II.

Going along this way I worked my way through, and the more recent the decade the harder it was for me to have an image of it. That is, I even forget if Lorrie Moore, say, is in the seventies or the eighties. I can't give you a pocket summary of what's happening in the short story now, except that people like Alice Munro and Lorrie Moore and Thom Jones are writing longer, attempting to expand the short story and to let in a little more novelistic largeness, to get many things going. The form is far from dying. What may be dying are the markets that can support or have supported short-story writers. But it's a very natural form, perhaps somewhat indigenous to the United States. Something about our lifestyle, our attention span, the pragmatic way we see experience in small bits and only look three yards ahead of us as we ski down the mountain. All this maybe helps to make us a nation in which the short story is a congenial form. It has energy and compression, and a little bit of what Fitzgerald says about Gatsby, the way he perches on the dashboard of his convertible with a resourcefulness of movement that comes from "the formless grace of our nervous, sporadic games." The English don't have anything like our tradition of short-story masters, which has elevated some short-story writers like Hawthorne and Poe and Ambrose Bierce to the status of major masters.

SCHIFF

I have one final question, then we'll take questions from the audience. We need to conclude in about twenty minutes because a journalist from the *Cincinnati Enquirer* is waiting in the wings—believe it or not—to interview John Updike. I'd like to end my part with a Rabbit question—namely, What was it like writing a Rabbit novel, or a novella in this case, without Rabbit? The second part of the question relates to our earlier discussion concerning genre. "Rabbit Remembered" is a novella, yet it's approximately the same number of pages, one hundred and eighty-five, as your first novel, *The Poorhouse Fair*. What makes this a novella and *The Poorhouse Fair* a novel?

A Conversation at the College Conservatory of Music

The Poorhouse Fair is a novel because, well, the bottom line is because I say it is. But it does have a multiplicity of characters and a complicated action to a degree, and certainly is not a novella in my book. I wanted to not write another Rabbit novel. I had written four about his life and death, and I thought that the tetralogy should be given the dignity of a beginning and ending—that there should not be an afterthought. Yet I had these afterthoughts, about his children, mostly, and, to some extent, the fate of his widow; there was a kind of Rabbit family. And after ten years I was still kicking as a writer, and I thought it would do no real harm to the Rabbit novels if I created a postscript. And although it did get to be, as Jim says, longish, it still is in my mind a short story. A short story revolving around the question: What do you do when you're forty years old and a sister you never knew you had shows up? Nelson's reaction is to want to take care of her, which, in the limited horizons of eastern Pennsylvania, means to get her married. At least he feels responsibility for her; he undertakes, in a sense, his father's role. And Rabbit is present in this novella as a memory that the characters share—they all have their own memories—but also as some kind of a living presence, genetic at the least, but maybe ghostly as well, in a sense supervising the action. So that was my thought. Whether I succeeded or not I can't say, but it felt, Jim, it felt nice to be back in Rabbit's Pennsylvania once again. It's a territory that shaped me, and though I left it fifty years ago to go to college, whenever I've located one of these Rabbit fictions in it, it comes alive for me. I seem to know how the people think. I seem to know what kind of things can happen and can't happen there. I don't have that feeling in my adopted territory of New England; I'm still a visitor, a tourist of sorts. So that each time I've gone back to the Rabbit series, there's been this kind of "Welcome Home!" feeling for me. I think I've probably gone as far with that as I can. Ten years from now, nine years from now, I can't imagine there being anything more left in Rabbit than a very short story.

SCHIFF

Let's turn now to questions from the audience.

AUDIENCE

How does your early notion of writing as an antidote to impermanence hold up at this stage in your writing?

UPDIKE

How have my early ideas of writing as an antidote to impermanence held up? Well, like everything you achieve, it loses a little of its shine. On the other hand, you would not want to not be in print. Is that right? I would not want to not be in print, right. I am happy, in short, to be in print. I still go at it with enthusiasm. It takes some patience and some juice to get going on a longer fiction. If you've done it often enough you know how much research and how many quizzical spots there will be where you don't quite know what the word is, or what the event would be. So it's a bit daunting each time. But what gets you up onto this pitch of wanting to do it, I think, is a vision of the finished book. The finished book on a shelf somewhere, available, permanent more or less.

It's being able to envision the words in type that still excites me enough that I keep writing. You might say, "Well, keep writing, what else are you going to do, you silly old fellow?" And it's true that it's become a habit, and unless I can secrete a certain amount of my particular poison each day I feel restless and irritated. But more than, I think, just a bad habit that I can't shake, it's the possibility of saying something that hasn't quite been said, and of saying it in such a way that it can't be said better. That's still an irresistible idea to me. So I think my childish instincts were basically sound.

A Conversation at the College Conservatory of Music

You mentioned Hawthorne as a major master of the short story, and you've written three versions of *The Scarlet Letter* from different points of view. But what about Hawthorne as a writer of tales or short pieces most attracts you? Or what kind of influence, if you will, has Hawthorne had?

UPDIKE

Hawthorne is an instructive case in the saga of the American short story because, as you know, he for a long time wrote only tales, and tales of a peculiarly delicate and elusive substance. It seems that Hawthorne could only write on the edge of parable, on the edge of allegory. Real life was something that the English could do. Trollope could do it but not Hawthorne. There are letters Hawthorne wrote to various people—I just read one the other day, written to someone you would know, I think Oliver Wendell Holmes or some other writer, complaining that he just couldn't do anything more than what he was doing with these kind of evanescent, delicate, elusive works. And I think it's the weakness of Hawthorne that he has this automatic recourse to the symbolic. So that even in *The Scarlet Letter,* which is his most triumphant piece of imagining—he had strong feelings about his Puritan ancestors and was able to conjure up that world and gave us the first American heroine and still one of the best American heroines—there's an awful lot of fiddling with the scarlet letter, with the symbol of the A, with the stars spelling out the A, with Dimmesdale's wounds, and with all kinds of what seems unnecessary folderol.

But that's America, I've decided. That is, we don't have the kind of brimming social structure that produces a Trollope or a Dickens. In theory we don't have classes. Now, in practice there are classes, and somebody like Dreiser can write quite compellingly about class struggle, and getting out of your class into a better one. But we're not accessible to each other imaginatively the way that the English and the French seem to be. For one thing, there's prudery about sexual matters; we don't have the kind of novel the French have been producing since Madame de Lafayette. There's no equivalent to the cold-eyed psychology that the French can bring to human relations.

So what do we have in America? We have these glimpses, these spiritually based moments of a kind of penetrating ghostliness. I don't know. But Hawthorne and Poe write stories on the edge of the unreal, as if the whole continent is on the edge of the unreal, and that we—at least in their generation and maybe even up to ours—haven't quite worked our way into the ground. We didn't have a Middle Ages, and that may matter. At any rate, Henry James and others have felt obliged to go to Europe to find suitable substance. To James almost everything American was so boring—you can just see the yawn in his prose. Willam Dean Howells tried to make it interesting. He said, "No, there's nothing intrinsically boring or elusive about American experience." Yet look who is the champion at the bookstores now and in the English courses: it's James and not poor Howells, who had such talent and was so devoted to ordinary life in America. Hawthorne was one of the first canaries that began to faint in the peculiar mine of the American consciousness. And I think he's with us, we love him still because of this, because of his sense of the unreal, the thing seen out of the side of your eye instead of the thing posed right in front of you and written about.

Tom Wolfe, the younger, the live Tom Wolfe keeps hammering away at the idea that we must go out, we writers, and confront American reality so rich in its diversity and so dynamic in its struggles and its wonderful capitalist, economic hurly-burly blah blah. And what do you get for all this—you get *A Man in Full,* which feels, for all of its virtues and its very significant journalistic interests, cooked up and hokey on some deep level that Hawthorne is not.

Could you talk a little bit about deciding to write *Gertrude and Claudius* and what that process was like?

I wrote *Gertrude and Claudius* because for some time I've had the feeling that Gertrude is, perhaps, the most appealing character in *Hamlet*. She has very few lines to say and yet everything she does say is kind of wonderful and to the point. "The lady doth protest too much" is one remark. "More matter, with less art" is another. And of death, "Thou know'st 'tis common—all that lives must die, / Passing through nature to eternity." So we have the impression of a majestic, stately, humane woman, quite queenly, innately queenly. Now, where does that leave Hamlet's question of "How could my mother have married this rascal with my father's body scarcely cold in the grave?" I tried to imagine the events before *Hamlet* that would give some plausibility to the wild aftermath that Shakespeare only lightly sketches.

It's a masterpiece, of course. It's the most loved, I suppose, and the most played of Shakespeare's plays. It's also, I think, an especially sloppy piece of work, as T. S. Eliot and others have pointed out. There's much that is hasty and illogical. Even the weather in *Hamlet* is kind of screwy: you go from bitter cold on the battlements to May and June flowers Ophelia is gathering within a few months. As theater, it gets by, but just barely. Shakespeare obviously did work under pressure, trying to please the actors and the managers and the groundlings and the sophisticates, and he did it. He made masterpieces. But certainly the events of *Hamlet*, if taken seriously, need some further explaining, and I tried to provide it.

Of course, I write out of a twentieth-century—a twenty-first-century sensibility now. Making Gertrude an unhappy wife, an unsatisfied wife, and furthermore a woman to whom motherhood has been a disappoint-ment—a little like Madame Bovary in that regard, in that the maternal glands failed to fully kick in, Hamlet being a difficult and even displeas-ing child—seemed to be my way of making sense of it. It is, of course, a certain retelling of the Hamlet legend, which has roots that go back at least to the eighth and ninth century, just as Shakespeare was retelling what had been even in his lifetime an oft-told tale. I felt there was some-thing there which needed to be explicated and needed to be brought out. It goes back to really a kind of a love, a love I felt for Gertrude as she appears in that play.

And what got me moving on it finally was seeing the four-hour Ken-neth Branagh movie of *Hamlet*, where you get the full script, plus Yorick and King Hamlet when alive. It emboldened me to tackle *Hamlet* at last. It was . . . I was about to say fun to do. It wasn't *only* fun to do. It did involve a little research, but a lot of it had to be bluffed, and my Middle Ages is a kind of generalized Middle Ages. It's not a historical novel the way a real historical novelist does them.

SCHIFF

Last question, in the back, Rob.

AUDIENCE

You've given us the "allegedly" *Best American Short Stories of the Cen-tury*, as you called it last night, and I'm just wondering if we will see a selected or collected *John Updike Short Stories* in the future. And if the former, if it were selected, which ones would you want to draw our at-tention to beyond "A&P"?

UPDIKE

I think you all heard that, or I hope you all heard that. Yes, I'm at that age when people do their own collections or selections. I'm between

A Conversation at the College Conservatory of Music

stools on it. Some of the books are still in print, others are not, but all are available in libraries if anybody really cares. John Cheever allowed his stories to be collected at a point when they were all out of print. And he just submitted to the process, as far as I know; I'm not even sure if John read proof on that book, which made such a success. Knopf, the publisher, has hopes perhaps of making a similar success out of mine, but I don't think it would work that way. The Cheever stories had a kind of Christmas gift look to them, and there were enough to make a big book, but not enough to make a daunting or an unpleasantly large book. I don't want to go through my stories separating sheep from goats. I don't want to. These were stories which all saw print. I put them all in books. I cared for them enough to put them in print, in a book. I've made my rejections of stories that didn't work out already, so I would want to just do a collection.

But the collection would be a little like the collected Pritchett stories or the William Trevor collection—books too big to hold. And what purpose do they serve? They compel a lot of reviewers to read them and write an essay about the short-story writer, but do they really enhance anybody's reading pleasure? So, I'm not quite that desperate, as if the only way I can produce a book is to produce an anthology, a collection of myself. But if I did, I think I would break them into two halves, the first ending somewhere around '75 or '76, and call it *Earlier Stories*. However, the order presents another problem. The stories were not published in strictly chronological order. Do I want to rearrange them? Is there any virtue in that, or is it mere scholarly vanity? Vanity, vanity— what isn't vanity in the literary game anyway? There are a number of stray stories. There's a story called "The Lucid Eye in Silver Town" that's really a pretty good story, but somehow it got left out of a collection and I put it in *Assorted Prose*. And a series of ten called *Interviews with Insufficiently Famous Americans*. And what of the Henry Bech stories, that already have their own collection, in Everyman? So I have all kinds of decisions to make that I'm not ready to face. Thank you.

SCHIFF

Thank you, John.

A Conversation at the College Conservatory of Music

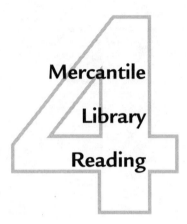

Mercantile
Library
Reading

Wednesday, April 18, 2001, at 6:30 p.m.

Fiction reading before a sold-out audience of two hundred

ALBERT PYLE, EXECUTIVE DIRECTOR OF THE MERCANTILE LIBRARY

Welcome to this final night in the 2001 Winter Author Series here at the Mercantile Library. I have a special announcement to make. On this day, April 18, 1835, the Mercantile Library was organized. This is our birthday. We are 166 years old today. There is no more appropriate way to celebrate the birthday than the way we are doing it tonight. The Mercantile Library was organized to improve its members and to improve the city, and this is exactly the kind of work we are happiest doing. We have been overwhelmed with the reaction to the Winter Author Series. Those of you who are involved in this kind of work know it is impossible without certain kinds of help. I'd like to recognize and thank our series sponsors, the Lois and Richard Rosenthal Foundation, and our event sponsor, Schiff Kreidler-Shell. We are happy and fortunate to have them with the series. We are, of course, delighted to have Jim Schiff, vice president of the Mercantile Library and a professor of English at the University of Cincinnati. We would not be here tonight with this particular author if it were not for the happy convergence of goals between the Mercantile Library and the University of Cincinnati and its Short Story Festival, on which Jim has labored long and hard. So we are very glad that that connection was made, and we thank you, Jim.

JAMES SCHIFF

Thank you, Albert, and thanks to everyone for coming out tonight and making this the fastest sellout in Library history. Through my involvement with the Library over the last decade, I've had many interesting and peculiar duties, though none more unexpected than that which occurred last night at Brooks Brothers around six o'clock. I should add— and my wife is here and will vouch for this—that I have never, in any manner, been known for my fashion sense. However, there I was, sorting through a rack of neckties, pulling out several, holding them up to the gray pinstripe suit that John Updike was wearing. An hour before he was to appear on stage at UC, John informed me that he had forgotten to pack his necktie. I don't recall ever helping someone shop for a necktie, so I felt gratified when John voiced satisfaction, even slight flattery, at my first several selections. I even began to feel, despite my wife's reservations, that perhaps I harbored a hidden talent here. However, I soon discovered that all the ties I had selected, John was quietly dropping into the rejection pile. Alas, my secret talent was not real. Nevertheless, in the process I discovered that John Updike is a kind and generous man, and I hope, if you get the chance, that you will compliment him on his tie.

John Updike spoke here at the Library approximately ten years ago. In fact, he read, among other pieces, his story, "The Rumor," which is

set in Cincinnati. The evening was so successful and our guest so eloquent that many of us felt strongly that we must have him back. Ten
years and thirteen books later, he has returned, and we are again delighted. As most of you know, John Updike is a writer whose list of accomplishments is impressive. He is the recipient on more than one occasion of the Pulitzer Prize and the National Book Critics Circle Award,
and he has also won the National Book Award and the Howells Medal.
His five-volume Rabbit saga may well be one of the major works of the
twentieth century. In fact, Rabbit Angstrom has become a kind of icon
in American literature. His death at the conclusion of *Rabbit at Rest* was
so momentous that both the *New York Times* and the *Washington Post*
addressed it not only in their book review sections but on their editorial pages as well. I cannot think of another fictional character in recent
American literature whose death, or life, has drawn this kind of attention. And what is interesting about these editorials is that they both treat
Rabbit as a real person, someone these journalists knew.

While John Updike is known widely for his nineteen novels, he has
also published over thirty-five hundred pages of literary criticism, seven
volumes of poetry, and more than two hundred short stories. His short
fiction—and I'm thinking particularly of the montage stories at the end
of *Pigeon Feathers,* the lyrical pieces in *The Music School,* the emotionally
resonant Maple stories in *Too Far to Go,* and the hilarious Bech tales gathered together now in *The Complete Henry Bech*—display the range, inven-
tiveness, and sheer brilliance of one of the great American short-story
writers of our time. Please welcome John Updike.

JOHN UPDIKE

Thank you. This is my Cincinnati tie. I'll wear it proudly wherever I
go now. Always when you pack, I find, there's one thing you've left out.
It never was a tie before this occasion, and I discovered it quite late, actually, not quite an hour before I was supposed to read. And I wasn't

sure the stores would be open, and I might have to borrow Jim's tie, or make a tie out of a pair of my underpants. But in fact he led me, unerringly, to Brooks Brothers, where I did dither a bit over what tie, there were so many lovely ones. I was drawn to a table that said "40 percent Off." Yet when I selected this conservative tie, that goes nicely with both white and blue, the bill was between, I hate to tell you this, fifty and sixty dollars. So I said to the young man, "Isn't there a 40 percent discount which you've forgotten?" And he just looked sort of starry-eyed and said nothing. So I think I was cheated. But I don't blame any of you.

One never knows quite what to read. I am here to celebrate the art of the short story, and I thought I would read one short story to you. No poems, no remarks, no jokes, no nothing, just read the story. It is a story that, speaking of prizes, did win a First O. Henry Prize. And it's present in this quite new book for me, *The Complete Henry Bech,* which contains twenty stories, some of them of novella length, about an alter ego who is not Rabbit Angstrom but Henry Bech, a New York, Jewish, nonproductive, bachelor writer. I invented him because years—decades—ago I had some experiences as a cultural ambassador to the then-Communist world that could have happened only to a writer on the road. So I had to invent a writer, and I tried to make him as little like myself as I could. At his core, however, he and I are twins. Twin writers.

I reread this story recently. I hope it needs no extensive explanation for those of you who are too young to remember the Cold War. But looking over the crowd, I think there are a few Cold War veterans here who can remember 1964. Khrushchev was excused from power while I was in the Soviet Union, and I was going to meet him, and never did. Never did. The course of history might have been changed. I also noticed the word "Negro" used in a couple places here. But it was the word of correct use at the time, and one can't keep up with the changing vocabulary of politically correct English. So I've left it in.

Mercantile Library Reading

The story is called "The Bulgarian Poetess." This was the story in which I invented Henry Bech, and I liked him so well that I went on to write nineteen more stories about him. I've written more stories about Bech than anybody else. He became, as a writer, a kind of device whereby I could vent my writerly feelings and my writerly experiences. And he becomes increasingly willful and fantastic. But he's quite a pussycat in this story, and you need not be afraid of him. He's soft and innocent—sort of like me.

The Bulgarian Poetess

"Your poems. Are they difficult?"

She smiled and, unaccustomed to speaking English, answered carefully, drawing a line in the air with two delicately pinched fingers holding an imaginary pen. "They are difficult—to write."

He laughed, startled and charmed. "But not to read?"

She seemed puzzled by his laugh, but did not withdraw her smile, though its corners deepened in a defensive, feminine way. "I think," she said, "not so very."

"Good." Brainlessly he repeated "Good," disarmed by her unexpected quality of truth. He was, himself, a writer, this forty-ish young man, Henry Bech, with his thinning curly hair and melancholy Jewish nose, the author of one good book and three others, the good one having come first. By a kind of oversight, he had never married. His reputation had grown while his powers declined. As he felt himself sink, in his fiction, deeper and deeper into eclectic sexuality and bravura narcissism, as his search for plain truth carried him farther and farther into treacherous realms of fantasy and, lately, of silence, he was more and more thickly hounded by homage, by flat-footed exegetes, by arrogantly worshipful undergraduates who had hitchhiked a thousand miles to touch his hand, by querulous translators, by election to honorary societies, by invitations to lecture, to "speak," to "read," to participate in symposia trumped up by ambitious girlie magazines in shameless

Updike in Cincinnati

conjunction with venerable universities. His very government, in airily unstamped envelopes from Washington, invited him to travel, as an ambassador of the arts, to the other half of the world, the hostile, mysterious half. Rather automatically, but with some faint hope of shaking himself loose from the burden of himself, he consented, and found himself floating, with a passport so stapled with visas it fluttered when pulled from his pocket, down into the dim airports of Communist cities.

He arrived in Sofia the day after a mixture of Bulgarian and African students had smashed the windows of the American legation and ignited an overturned Chevrolet. The cultural officer, pale from a sleepless night of guard duty, tamping his pipe with trembling fingers, advised Bech to stay out of crowds and escorted him to his hotel. The lobby was swarming with Negroes in black wool fezzes and pointed European shoes. Insecurely disguised, he felt, by an astrakhan hat purchased in Moscow, Bech passed through to the elevator, whose operator addressed him in German. *"Ja, vier,"* Bech answered, *"danke,"* and telephoned, in his bad French, for dinner to be brought up to his room. He remained there all night, behind a locked door, reading Hawthorne. He had lifted a paperback collection of short stories from a legation windowsill littered with broken glass. A few curved bright crumbs fell from between the pages onto his blanket. The image of Roger Malvin lying alone, dying, in the forest—"Death would come like the slow approach of a corpse, stealing gradually towards him through the forest, and showing its ghastly and motionless features from behind a nearer and yet a nearer tree"—frightened him. Bech fell asleep early and suffered from swollen, homesick dreams. It had been the first day of Hanukkah.

In the morning, venturing downstairs for breakfast, he was surprised to find the restaurant open, the waiters affable, the eggs actual, the coffee hot, though syrupy. Outside, Sofia was sunny and (except for a few dark glances at his big American shoes) amenable to his passage along the streets. Lozenge-patterns of pansies, looking flat and brittle as pressed flowers, had been set

Mercantile Library Reading

in the public beds. Women with a touch of Western chic walked hatless in the park behind the mausoleum of Georgi Dimitrov. There was a mosque, and an assortment of trolley cars salvaged from the remotest corner of Bech's childhood, and a tree that talked—that is, it was so full of birds that it swayed under their weight and emitted volumes of chirping sound like a great leafy loudspeaker. It was the inverse of his hotel, whose silent walls presumably contained listening microphones. Electricity was somewhat enchanted in the Socialist world. Lights flickered off untouched and radios turned themselves on. Telephones rang in the dead of the night and breathed wordlessly in his ear. Six weeks ago, flying from New York City, Bech had expected Moscow to be a blazing counterpart and instead saw, through the plane window, a skein of hoarded lights no brighter, on that vast black plain, than a girl's body in a dark room.

Past the talking tree stood the American legation. The sidewalk, heaped with broken glass, was roped off, so that pedestrians had to detour into the gutter. Bech detached himself from the stream, crossed the little barren of pavement, smiled at the Bulgarian militiamen who were sullenly guarding the jewel-bright heaps of shards, and pulled open the bronze door. The cultural officer was crisper after a normal night's sleep. He clenched his pipe in his teeth and handed Bech a small list. "You're to meet with the Writers' Union at eleven. These are writers you might ask to see. As far as we can tell, they're among the more progressive."

Words like "progressive" and "liberal" had a somewhat reversed sense in this world. At times, indeed, Bech felt he had passed through a mirror, a dingy flecked mirror that reflected feebly the capitalist world; in its dim depths everything was similar but left-handed. One of the names ended in "-ova." Bech said, "A woman."

"A poetess," the cultural officer said, sucking and tamping in a fury of bogus efficiency. "Very popular, apparently. Her books are impossible to buy."

"Have you read anything by these people?"

Updike in Cincinnati

"I'll be frank with you. I can just about make my way through a newspaper."

"But you always know what a newspaper will say anyway."

"I'm sorry, I don't get your meaning."

"There isn't any." Bech didn't quite know why the Americans he met here behind the mirror irritated him—whether because they garishly refused to blend into this shadow-world or because they were always so solemnly sending him on ridiculous errands.

AT THE WRITERS' UNION, he handed the secretary the list as it had been handed to him, on U.S. legation stationery. The secretary, a large stooped man with the hands of a stonemason, grimaced and shook his head but obligingly reached for the telephone. Bech's meeting was already waiting in another room. It was the usual one, the one that, with small differences, he had already attended in Moscow and Kiev, Yerevan and Alma-Ata, Bucharest and Prague: the polished oval table, the bowl of fruit, the morning light, the gleaming glasses of brandy and mineral water, the lurking portrait of Lenin, the six or eight patiently sitting men who would leap to their feet with quick blank smiles. These men would include a few literary officials, termed "critics," high in the Party, loquacious and witty and destined to propose a toast to international understanding; a few selected novelists and poets, mustachioed, smoking, sulking at this invasion of their time; a university professor, the head of the Anglo-American Literature department, speaking in a beautiful withered English of Mark Twain and Sinclair Lewis; a young interpreter with a moist handshake; a shaggy old journalist obsequiously scribbling notes; and, on the rim of the group, in chairs placed to suggest that they had invited themselves, one or two gentlemen of ill-defined status, fidgety and tieless, maverick translators who would turn out to be the only ones present who had ever read a word by Henry Bech.

Here this type was represented by a stout man in a tweed coat leather-patched at the elbows in the British style. The whites of his eyes were distinctly red. He shook Bech's hand eagerly, made of it

Mercantile Library Reading

almost an embrace of reunion, bending his face so close that Bech could distinguish the smells of tobacco, garlic, cheese, and alcohol. Even as they were seating themselves around the table, and the Writers' Union chairman, a man elegantly bald, with very pale eyelashes, was touching his brandy glass as if to lift it, this anxious red-eyed interloper blurted at Bech, "Your *Travel Light* was so marvellous a book. The motels, the highways, the young girls with their lovers who were motorcyclists, so marvellous, so American, the youth, the adoration for space and speed, the barbarity of the advertisements in neon lighting, the very poetry. It takes us truly into another dimension."

Travel Light was the first novel, the famous one. Bech disliked discussing it. "At home," he said, "it was criticized as despairing."

The man's hands, stained orange with tobacco, lifted in amazement and plopped noisily to his knees. "No, no a thousand times. Truth, wonder, terror even, vulgarity, yes. But despair, no, not at all, not one iota. Your critics are dead wrong."

"Thank you."

The chairman softly cleared his throat and lifted his glass an inch from the table, so that it formed with its reflection a kind of playing card.

Bech's admirer excitedly persisted. "You are not a *wet* writer, no. You are a dry writer, yes? You have the expressions, am I wrong in English, dry, hard?"

"More or less."

"I want to translate you!"

It was the agonized cry of a condemned man, for the chairman coldly lifted his glass to the height of his eyes, and like a firing squad the others followed suit. Blinking his white lashes, the chairman gazed mistily in the direction of the sudden silence, and spoke in Bulgarian.

The young interpreter murmured in Bech's ear. "I wish to propose now, ah, a very brief toast. I know it will seem doubly brief to our honored American guest, who has so recently enjoyed the, ah, hospitality of our Soviet comrades." There must have been a

Updike in Cincinnati

joke here, for the rest of the table laughed. "But in seriousness permit me to say that in our country we have seen in years past too few Americans, ah, of Mr. Bech's progressive and sympathetic stripe. We hope in the next hour to learn from him much that is interesting and, ah, socially useful about the literature of his large country, and perhaps we may in turn inform him of our own proud literature, of which perhaps he knows regrettably little. Ah, so let me finally, then, since there is a saying that too long a courtship spoils the marriage, offer to drink, in our native plum brandy *slivovica*, ah, firstly to the success of his visit and, in the second place, to the mutual increase of international understanding."

"Thank you," Bech said and, as a courtesy, drained his glass. It was wrong; the others, having merely sipped, stared. The purple burning revolved in Bech's stomach, and a severe distaste—for himself, for his role, for this entire artificial and futile process—lighted upon a small brown spot on a pear in the bowl so shiningly posed before his eyes.

The red-eyed fool smelling of cheese was ornamenting the toast. "It is a personal honor for me to meet the man who, in *Travel Light,* truly added a new dimension to American prose."

"The book was written," Bech said, "ten years ago."

"And since?" A slumping, mustached man sat up and sprang into English. "Since, you have written what?"

Bech had been asked that question often in these weeks and his answer had grown curt. "A second novel called *Brother Pig,* which is St. Bernard's expression for the body."

"Good. Yes, and?"

"A collection of essays and sketches called *When the Saints.*"

"I like the title less well."

"It's the beginning of a famous Negro song."

"We know the song," another man said, a smaller man, with the tense, dented mouth of a hare. He lightly sang, "Lordy, I just want to be in that number."

"And the last book," Bech said, "was a long novel called *The Chosen* that took five years to write and that nobody liked."

"I have read reviews," the red-eyed man said. "I have not read the book. Copies are difficult here."

"I'll give you one," Bech said.

The promise seemed, somehow, to make the recipient unfortunately conspicuous; wringing his stained hands, he appeared to swell in size, to intrude grotesquely upon the inner ring, so that the interpreter took it upon himself to whisper, with the haste of an apology, into Bech's ear, "This gentleman is well known as the translator into our language of *Alice in Wonderland.*"

"A marvellous book," the translator said, deflating in relief, pulling at his pockets for a cigarette. "It truly takes us into another dimension. Something that must be done. We live in a new cosmos."

The chairman spoke in Bulgarian, musically, at length. There was polite laughter. Nobody translated for Bech. The professorial type, his black hair as rigid as a toupee, jerked forward. "Tell me, is it true, as I have read"—his phrases whistled slightly, like rusty machinery—"that the stock of Sinclair Lewis has plummeted under the Salinger wave?"

And so it went, here as in Kiev, Prague, and Alma-Ata, the same questions, more or less predictable, and his own answers, terribly familiar to him by now, mechanical, stale, irrelevant, untrue, claustrophobic. Then the door opened. In came, with the rosy air of a woman fresh from a bath, a little breathless, having hurried, hatless, a woman in a blond coat, her hair also blond. The secretary, entering behind her, seemed to make a cherishing space around her with his large curved hands. He introduced her to Bech as Vera Something-ova, the poetess he had asked to meet. None of the others on the list, he explained, answered their telephones.

"Aren't you kind to come?" As Bech asked it, it was a genuine question, to which he expected some sort of an answer.

She spoke to the interpreter in Bulgarian. "She says," the interpreter told Bech, "she is sorry she is so late."

"But she was just called!" In the warmth of his confusion and pleasure Bech turned to speak directly to her, forgetting he would not be understood. "I'm terribly sorry to have interrupted your morning."

"I am pleased," she said, "to meet you. I heard of you spoken in France."

"You speak English!"

"No. Very little amount."

"But you *do.*"

A chair was brought for her from a corner of the room. She yielded her coat, revealing herself in a suit also blond, as if her clothes were an aspect of a total consistency. She sat down opposite Bech, crossing her legs. Her legs were visibly good; her face was perceptibly broad. Lowering her lids, she tugged her skirt to the curve of her knee. It was his sense of her having hurried, hurried to him, and of being, still, graciously flustered, that most touched him.

He spoke to her very clearly, across the fruit, fearful of abusing and breaking the fragile bridge of her English. "You are a poetess. When I was young, I also wrote poems."

She was silent so long he thought she would never answer; but then she smiled and pronounced, "You are not old now."

"Your poems. Are they difficult?"

"They are difficult—to write."

"But not to read?"

"I think—not so very."

"Good. Good."

Despite the decay of his career, Bech had retained an absolute faith in his instincts; he never doubted that somewhere an ideal course was open to him and that his intuitions were predealt clues to his destiny. He had loved, briefly or long, with or without consummation, perhaps a dozen women; yet all of them, he now saw, shared the trait of approximation, of narrowly missing an undisclosed prototype. The surprise he felt did not have to do with the appearance, at last, of this central woman; he had always expected her to appear. What he had not expected was her appearance here, in this remote and bullied nation, in this room of morning light, where he discovered a small knife in his fingers and on the table before him, golden and moist, a precisely divided pear.

MEN TRAVELLING ALONE develop a romantic vertigo. Bech had already fallen in love with a freckled embassy wife in Prague, a buck-toothed chanteuse in Romania, a stolid Mongolian sculptress in Kazakhstan. In the Tretyakov Gallery he had fallen in love with a recumbent statue, and at the Moscow Ballet School with an entire roomful of girls. Entering the room, he had been struck by the aroma, tenderly acrid, of young female sweat. Sixteen and seventeen, wearing patchy practice suits, the girls were twirling so strenuously their slippers were unravelling. Demure student faces crowned the unconscious insolence of their bodies. The room was doubled in depth by a floor-to-ceiling mirror. Bech was seated on a bench at its base. Staring above his head, each girl watched herself with frowning eyes frozen, for an instant in the turn, by the imperious delay and snap of her head. Bech tried to remember the lines of Rilke that expressed it, this snap and delay: *did not the drawing remain / that the dark stroke of your eyebrow / swiftly wrote on the wall of its own turning?* At one point the teacher, a shapeless old Ukrainian lady with gold canines, a *prima* of the Thirties, had arisen and cried something translated to Bech as, "No, no, the arms free, *free!*" And in demonstration she had executed a rapid series of pirouettes with such proud effortlessness that all the girls, standing this way and that like deer along the wall, had applauded. Bech had loved them for that. In all his loves, there was an urge to rescue—to rescue the girls from the slavery of their exertions, the statue from the cold grip of its own marble, the embassy wife from her boring and unctuous husband, the chanteuse from her nightly humiliation (she could not sing), the Mongolian from her stolid race. But the Bulgarian poetess presented herself to him as needing nothing, as being complete, poised, satisfied, achieved. He was aroused and curious and, the next day, inquired about her of the man with the vaguely contemptuous mouth of a

Updike in Cincinnati

hare—a novelist turned playwright and scenarist, who accompanied him to the Rila Monastery. "She lives to write," the playwright said. "I do not think it is healthy."

Bech said, "But she seems so healthy." They stood beside a small church with whitewashed walls. From the outside it looked like a hovel, a shelter for pigs or chickens. For five centuries the Turks had ruled Bulgaria, and the Christian churches, however richly adorned within, had humble exteriors. A peasant woman with wildly snarled hair unlocked the door for them. Though the church could hardly ever have held more than fifty worshippers, it was divided into three parts, and every inch of wall was covered with eighteenth-century frescoes. Those in the narthex depicted a Hell where the devils wielded scimitars. Passing through the tiny nave, Bech peeked through the iconostasis into the screened area that, in the symbolism of Orthodox architecture, represented the next, the hidden world—Paradise. He glimpsed a row of books, an easy chair, a pair of ancient oval spectacles. Outdoors again, he felt released from the unpleasantly tight atmosphere of a children's book. They were on the side of a hill. Above them was a stand of pines whose trunks wore shells of ice. Below them sprawled the monastery, a citadel of Bulgarian national feeling during the years of the Turkish Yoke. The last monks had been moved out in 1961. An aimless soft rain was falling in these mountains, and there were not many German tourists today. Across the valley, whose little silver river still turned a water wheel, a motionless white horse stood silhouetted against a green meadow, pinned there like a brooch.

"I am an old friend of hers," the playwright said. "I worry about her."

"Are the poems good?"

"It is difficult for me to judge. They are very feminine. Perhaps shallow."

"Shallowness can be a kind of honesty."

"Yes. She is very honest in her work."

"And in her life?"

"As well."

"What does her husband do?"

The other man looked at him with parted lips and touched his arm, a strange Slavic gesture, communicating an underlying racial urgency, that Bech no longer shied from. "But she has no husband. As I say, she is too much for poetry to have married."

"But her name ends in '-ova.'"

"I see. You are mistaken. It is not a matter of marriage; I am Petrov, my unmarried sister is Petrova. All females."

"How stupid of me. But I think it's such a pity, she's so charming."

"In America, only the uncharming fail to marry?"

"Yes, you must be very uncharming not to marry."

"It is not so here. The government indeed is alarmed; our birthrate is one of the lowest in Europe. It is a problem for economists."

Bech gestured at the monastery. "Too many monks?"

"Not enough, perhaps. With too few of monks, something of the monk enters everybody."

The peasant woman, who seemed old to Bech but who was probably younger than he, saw them to the edge of her domain. She huskily chattered in what Petrov said was very amusing rural slang. Behind her, now hiding in her skirts and now darting away, was her child, a boy not more than three. He was faithfully chased, back and forth, by a small white pig, who moved, as pigs do, on tiptoe, with remarkably abrupt changes of direction. Something in the scene, in the open glee of the woman's parting smile and the untamed way her hair thrust out from her head, something in the mountain mist and spongy rutted turf into which frost had begun to break at night, evoked for Bech a nameless absence to which was attached, like a horse to a meadow, the image of the poetess, with her broad face, her good legs, her Parisian clothes, and her sleekly brushed hair. Petrov, in whom he was beginning to sense, through the wraps of foreignness, a clever and kindred mind, seemed to have overheard his thoughts, for he said, "If you would like, we could have dinner. It would be easy for me to arrange."

"With her?"

"Yes, she is my friend, she would be glad."

"But I have nothing to say to her. I'm just curious about such an intense conjunction of good looks and brains. I mean, what does a soul do with it all?"

"You may ask her. Tomorrow night?"

"I'm sorry, I can't. I'm scheduled to go to the ballet, and the next night the legation is giving a cocktail party for me, and then I fly home."

"Home? So soon?"

"It does not feel soon to me. I must try to work again."

"A drink, then. Tomorrow evening before the ballet? It is possible? It is not possible."

Petrov looked puzzled, and Bech realized that it was his fault, for he was nodding to say Yes, but in Bulgaria nodding meant No, and a shake of the head meant Yes. "Yes," he said. "Gladly."

THE BALLET was entitled *Silver Slippers*. As Bech watched it, the word "ethnic" kept coming to his mind. He had grown accustomed, during his trip, to this sort of artistic evasion, the retreat from the difficult and disappointing present into folk dance, folk tale, folk song, with always the implication that, beneath the embroidered peasant costume, the folk was really one's heart's own darling, the proletariat.

"Do you like fairy tales?" It was the moist-palmed interpreter who accompanied him to the theatre.

"I *love* them," Bech said, with a fervor and gaiety lingering from the previous hour. The interpreter looked at him anxiously, as when Bech had swallowed the brandy in one swig, and throughout the ballet kept murmuring explanations of self-evident events on the stage. Each night, a princess would put on silver slippers and dance through her mirror to tryst with a wizard, who possessed a magic stick that she coveted, for with it the world could be ruled. The wizard, as a dancer, was inept, and once almost dropped her, so that anger flashed from her eyes. She was, the princess, a little redhead with a high round bottom and a frozen pout and beautiful free arm motions, and Bech found it oddly ecstatic when, preparatory to her leap, she could dance toward the mirror, an empty oval, and another girl, identically dressed in pink, would emerge from the wings and perform as her reflection. And when the princess, haughtily adjusting her cape of invisibility, leaped through the oval of gold wire, Bech's heart leaped backward into the enchanted hour he had spent with the poetess.

Though the appointment had been established, she came into the restaurant as if, again, she had been suddenly summoned and had hurried. She sat down between Bech and Petrov slightly breathless and fussed, but exuding, again, that impalpable warmth of intelligence and virtue.

"Vera, Vera," Petrov said.

"You hurry too much," Bech told her.

"Not so very much," she said.

Petrov ordered her a cognac and continued with Bech their discussion of the newer French novelists. "It is tricks," Petrov said. "Good tricks, but tricks. It does not have enough to do with life, it is too much verbal nervousness. Is that sense?"

"It's an epigram," Bech said.

"There are just two of their number with whom I do not feel this: Claude Simon and Samuel Beckett. You have no relation, Bech, Beckett?"

"None."

Vera said, "Nathalie Sarraute is a very modest woman. She felt motherly to me."

"You have met her?"

"In Paris I heard her speak. Afterward there was the coffee. I liked her theories, of the, oh, *what?* Of the *little* movements within the heart." She delicately measured a pinch of space and smiled, through Bech, back at herself.

"Tricks," Petrov said. "I do not feel this with Beckett; there, in a low form, believe it or not, one has human content."

Bech felt duty-bound to pursue this, to ask about the theatre of the absurd in Bulgaria, about abstract painting. These were the

Updike in Cincinnati

touchstones of American-style progressiveness; Russia had none, Romania some, Czechoslovakia plenty. Instead, he asked the poetess, "Motherly?"

Vera explained, her hands delicately modelling the air, rounding into nuance, as it were, the square corners of her words. "After her talk, we—talked."

"In French?"

"And in Russian."

"She knows Russian?"

"She was born Russian."

"How is her Russian?"

"Very pure but—old-fashioned. Like a book. As she talked, I felt in a book, safe."

"You do not always feel safe?"

"Not always."

"Do you find it difficult to be a woman poet?"

"We have a tradition of woman poets. We have Elisaveta Bagriyana, who is very great."

Petrov leaned toward Bech as if to nibble him. "Your own works? Are they influenced by the *nouvelle vague*? Do you consider yourself to write anti-*romans*?"

Bech kept himself turned toward the woman. "Do you want to hear about how I write? You don't, do you?"

"Very much yes," she said.

He told them, told them shamelessly, in a voice that surprised him with its steadiness, its limpid urgency, how once he had written, how in *Travel Light* he had sought to show people skimming the surface of things with their lives, taking tints from things the way that objects in a still life color one another, and how later he had attempted to place beneath the melody of plot a countermelody of imagery, interlocking images which had risen to the top and drowned his story, and how in *The Chosen* he had sought to make of this confusion the theme itself, an epic theme, by showing a population of characters whose actions were all determined, at the deepest level, by nostalgia, by a desire to get back, to dive, each, into the springs of their private imagery. The book probably failed; at least, it was badly received. Bech apologized for telling all this. His voice tasted flat in his mouth; he felt a secret intoxication and a secret guilt, for he had contrived to give a grand air, as of an impossibly noble and quixotically complex experiment, to his failure, when at bottom, he suspected, a certain simple laziness was the cause.

Petrov said, "Fiction so formally sentimental could not be composed in Bulgaria. We do not have a happy history."

It was the first time Petrov had sounded like a Communist. If there was one thing that irked Bech about these people behind the mirror, it was their assumption that, however second-rate elsewhere, in suffering they were supreme. He said, "Believe it or not, neither do we."

Vera calmly intruded. "Your personae are not moved by love?"

"Yes, very much. But as a form of nostalgia. We fall in love, I tried to say in the book, with women who remind us of our first landscape. A silly idea. I used to be interested in love. I once wrote an essay on the orgasm—you know the word?—"

She shook her head. He remembered that it meant Yes.

"—on the orgasm as perfect memory. The one mystery is, what are we remembering?"

She shook her head again, and he noticed that her eyes were gray, and that in their depths his image (which he could not see) was searching for the thing remembered. She composed her fingertips around the brandy glass and said, "There is a French poet, a young one, who has written of this. He says that never else do we, do we so gather up, collect into ourselves, oh—" Vexed, she spoke to Petrov in rapid Bulgarian.

He shrugged and said, "Concentrate our attention."

"—concentrate our attention," she repeated to Bech, as if the words, to be believed, had to come from her. "I say it foolish—foolishly—but in French it is very well put and—*correct.*"

Petrov smiled neatly and said, "This is an enjoyable subject for discussion, love."

Updike in Cincinnati

"It remains," Bech said, picking his words as if the language were not native even to him, "one of the few things that still warrant meditation."

"I think it is good," she said.

"Love?" he asked, startled.

She shook her head and tapped the stem of her glass with a fingernail, so that Bech had an inaudible sense of ringing, and she bent as if to study the liquor, so that her entire body borrowed a rosiness from the brandy and burned itself into Bech's memory— the silver gloss of her nail, the sheen of her hair, the symmetry of her arms relaxed on the white tablecloth, everything except the expression on her face.

Petrov asked aloud Bech's opinion of Dürrenmatt.

ACTUALITY IS a running impoverishment of possibility. Though he had looked forward to seeing her again at the legation cocktail party and had made sure that she was invited, when it occurred, though she came, he could not get to her. He saw her enter, with Petrov, but he was fenced in by an attaché of the Yugoslav Embassy and his burnished Tunisian wife; and, later, when he was worming his way toward her diagonally, a steely hand closed on his arm and a rasping American female told him that her fifteen-year-old nephew had decided to be a writer and desperately needed advice. Not the standard crap, but real brass-knuckles advice. Bech found himself balked. He was surrounded by America: the voices, the narrow suits, the watery drinks, the clatter, the glitter. The mirror had gone opaque and gave him back only himself. He managed, in the end, as the officials were thinning out, to break through and confront her in a corner. Her coat, blond, with a rabbit collar, was already on; from its side pocket she pulled a pale volume of poems in the Cyrillic alphabet. "Please," she said. On the flyleaf she had written, "to H. Beck, sincerelly, with bad spellings but much"—the last word looked like "leave" but must have been "love."

"Wait," he begged, and went back to where his ravaged pile of presentation books had been and, unable to find the one he wanted, stole the legation library's jacketless copy of *The Chosen*. Placing it in her expectant hands, he told her, "Don't look," for inside he had written, with a drunk's stylistic confidence,

Dear Vera Glavanakova—
It is a matter of earnest regret for me that you and I must live on opposite sides of the world.

JOHN UPDIKE

Thank you. That was a generous helping of Bech in the Communist world, but a few decades ago there certainly was an enchanted feeling of being behind the Iron Curtain if you were a good American. I know you all have things to do, meals to eat, and I don't want to run over my time. I'm sorry the story was as long as it was. I looked for passages to cut, and I couldn't find a word. But maybe we could have ten minutes of questions, if you have any questions. Yes, down here.

AUDIENCE

In one of your short stories, you say something like "Intimidation is 85 percent of human interaction." Or at least your character says that. And I'm wondering if that's the case, particularly as I get older, and whether that's something you believe too?

UPDIKE

The word is "intimidation"? "Intimidation is 85 percent of human interaction." I think Bech did say that somewhere, and I wouldn't give the lie to one of my own characters. They work hard for me and do their best. But I think, as in the animal world, we all need a certain space around us, otherwise we'll get crushed, and intimidation is one of the ways in which we maintain that space. As we walk down the street, and so on, a little intimidation is going on, a warning of limits. Like birdsong, like animal grunts and urine, we mark our territory and try to hold it. This is not necessarily a bad thing, except when it gets into the national scale, and goes wrong, and war results. But certainly international relations are, in part, a matter of intimidation also; it does not end with the human unit but extends into a scary global dimension as well.

Yes?

I have the May issue of the *Atlantic Monthly* here, in which Simon Winchester has written an article decrying the influences of *Roget's Thesaurus* on literature. Towards the end of the article, he writes, "I thought when I began this that I might telephone a writer representative, a few writers, to ask if they use *Roget* in any measurable degree. I'm wondering if I might drop a line to John Updike. In the end I neither called nor wrote because I knew the answer without him. Everyone has the book, occasionally one makes use of it, but one never relies on it to help with the making of good writing." Now my question is, Are you or were you ever in the habit of consulting *Roget's Thesaurus*?

Uh, yes. Since I'm under oath, I must say yes. I have a couple of them actually. I think I inherited one from my mother, she had a *Roget* and I used to look into it. I also have the later thesaurus wherein you can look up a word under its alphabetical entry, which is a little easier than the old *Roget* system of categories—a virtual cosmology of words which he arranged, and not always easy to find your way around in.

Of course, one doesn't want to write like a thesaurus. You generally go for the first word that occurs to you, and the most elementary Anglo-Saxon word is usually the best. But this is a large language, a mongrel language of many roots and synonyms, and so you have the feeling that for every phenomenon there probably is a word or expression if you can just think of it. Sometimes the thesaurus helps you find that word.

Often it doesn't. Often you seem to know more than the thesaurus. But I think you could say it's a harmless tool. I find in the matter of colors, I'm always looking for the names of shades of color. Somehow green, blue, red—they don't quite do it for me anymore, and I'm trying to be more precise, as a painter is. Sometimes the thesaurus does have just the expression you want. A very hard area for me, I'll confide to this audience, is eye color, since it turns out I rarely look people in the eye. I'm a shifty, shy boy who sort of shambles, and you may think I'm looking you in the eye, but I bet I could have a conversation with anybody here, and after, if you asked me what eye color you were, I wouldn't know. I don't even know my own father's eye color, although my mother always said it was yellow. Yellow eyes. So I've been trying to steel myself, to better myself as a writer by looking more into people's eyes. One thing I have noticed is that it's quite rare to see really black eyes; it's usually a shade of brown and sometimes a surprisingly light shade of brown, freckled brown, even in otherwise quite dark people. But yeah, sure, I use it. I use anything I can get my hands on to try to make the prose more precise and interesting. And sometimes it's the odd word that helps makes a sentence interesting.

Yes?

AUDIENCE

Would you comment on your changing use of names in your novel *Gertrude and Claudius*?

UPDIKE

I hope you could all hear that, it's about the change of names in a novel called *Gertrude and Claudius*. When I began to look into the sources of the Hamlet legend, I discovered that the Viking names were rather different. Gertrude was not Gertrude, but Gerutha, Geruthe—first with an A, then with an E. Hamlet began as Ambleth, his father was Hor-

Updike in Cincinnati

wendil, and Claudius was something quite other than Claudius—Feng, believe it or not. The old names helped me retell the legend in a layered way to indicate its deep roots in Viking mythology and in Viking habits. This is a story of deceit and revenge of a kind that even in Shakespeare's day was unusually brutal, but it was very much a part with the old Viking way of doing things. The earlier names, I thought, gave a touch of the archaic, and also demonstrated that I was trying to take the story back to its origins.

Gertrude was attractive to Claudius in part because she was herself a princess. She was, in my construction, the only child, the daughter of Rorik, and the man who won her would win the throne of Denmark. So all that seemed somehow to work better if I used the old names. I didn't think any essential confusion was created, although I did move what had been part of an afterword to the foreword so that the reader would be warned immediately that there would be some tricky stuff about names coming. I think the reader has to struggle enough, so that you should help him whenever you can without lowering yourself, or condescending to him or her, of course.

Yes, over here?

AUDIENCE

There was a criticism of Picasso, that at some point he just began making more Picassos and quit painting. Do you work hard to stay fresh and to keep from doing something, in your mind, that is another John Updike?

UPDIKE

It is true that everything you do turns out to be by John Updike, and that's a little disconcerting. Even though I stand back from it a few steps, I can see that, yes, I've done that before, or this is true, or this is a kind of tic of mine, or this an obsession of mine. Archaeology, for

Mercantile Library Reading

example. I read a story this afternoon—or whenever that was, maybe yesterday evening, the days and nights run together here in frenetic Cincinnati—in which certain themes recurred, like archaeology. But at least in the initial stage you *must* have the illusion that you're doing something you've never done before, and that it's a departure. *Gertrude and Claudius* was certainly a departure. The invention of Henry Bech was a departure for me. There must be some pinch of the undone, of the untried, to make it interesting enough for you to embark upon. But in the end, yes, in a strange way, just as you can tell a certain painter across the room, there is a kind of handwriting, a certain verbal handwriting that marks a thing as your own. It's something you can't be self-conscious about, but it does happen. In a way it's a limit, too. The more you write, the more you're in danger of revealing your limits, of showing you can only do X number of things instead of X and Y things.

One more question, if there is one. Maybe I've silenced all my critics. Yes, back there.

AUDIENCE

A distinguished writer has told us that the world craves book reviews far more than it craves books. That being so, would you care to speculate on the future of the actual book?

UPDIKE

Well, eventually the book will be replaced entirely by reviews of itself, and there will be no need to read the book at all. It's almost come to that. I think it was I who said that, wasn't it—that the world craves book reviews more than books? Nobody really invites me to write a book, or urges me to do it, or offers me any money to do it. I sit down and I do it because I feel I owe it to my talent and my audience, however modest it is. For the book reviews I do, on the other hand, there's quite a lively market. They provide the sensation of reading the book, and yet it's a way of not reading the book. As our attention spans shrink, book reviews offer a quick cultural fix.

I've written quite a few of them. They are in their way an art form, too—not to my mind a major art form, but we all live crowded lives full of many alternative entertainments than reading, and it's hard for us, even those of us who make our living in the trade, to get to the books we feel we should read. So book reviews in some sense ease our guilt, the print guilt that haunts us all. But not you, because you're such a loyal bookish audience and you showed up tonight, and I thank you. Thank you.

ALBERT PYLE

Thank you, Mr. Updike. Thank you, Jim, Lois, and Dick. Thank you all for coming. We do have copies of books for sale. Are you willing to do a little more signing?

UPDIKE

I'll sign a few.

PYLE

He'll sign a few. No more than two books per person, please. And be courteous with your time, as there are people in line. Thank you all for coming.